THE GLITCH

THE GLITCH

GRACE KWAK

NEW DEGREE PRESS

THE GLITCH

Cover Art: Digital hand designed by rawpixel.com / Freepik

ISBN   978-1-63730-685-7   *Paperback*

          978-1-63730-775-5   *Kindle Ebook*

          979-8-88504-031-0   *Ebook*

TABLE OF CONTENTS

"I have thrown away my lantern, and I can see the dark."

—WENDELL BARRY

NOTE FROM THE AUTHOR

——

As an engineering student, I'm always looking for ways to solve problems. Sometimes, my goal is to figure out how to make a software program more robust; other times, it's to make a circuit more efficient. Regardless of the application, there's an underlying principle in which the world is distilled into a collection of resources that follow very specific rules of math and physics, which can (and morally should) be harnessed in better ways. For the most part, I think this is all well and good; I mean, where would we be without technology, right?

But somewhere along the way, this mindset of relentless optimization seeped into the way I saw my life as a whole. In high school, I was the stereotypical Silicon Valley kid with eight million different productivity apps to optimize my day-to-day existence. I did get stuff done, but as you can imagine, it came with a cost.

For starters, whenever I found a better way of doing something, instead of feeling good about myself for improving and growing, a part of me felt resentment; why hadn't I thought of this before? How much time had I wasted because I hadn't known better? This is my first and last time being alive and every mistake I make brings me that much further away from reaching my highest potential. I didn't see the inherent value in the journey itself.

Because in engineering, whenever you make an error, you lose something, whether it's development time, hardware parts, or simply your own finite reservoir of energy. You do learn from your mistakes, but at best, that's a consolation prize; if you'd known everything to begin with and hadn't needed to make any errors in the first place, that would've been better. It makes sense in the context of a tech company, but it's not a good way to treat yourself, especially if you're an angsty teen.

What's more is that I became so focused on becoming this nebulous idea of the "optimal" Grace that I tried to strip away every part of myself that didn't fit with it. I was ashamed of the inconvenient and confusing parts of myself, and I thought I could use my shame to erase them from my identity. I tried to run away from my feelings because I thought they'd "get in the way." The field of engineering values rationality, progress, standardization, and control; it tries to eliminate the inexplicable, chaotic, blobby, and emotional.

But once I gave myself permission to value my so-called flaws or, dare I say, *glitches*, I bloomed. Since I no longer needed to justify my every decision, I was free to do whatever I wanted. I became happier, more confident, and more excited about the person I was and the person I would become. Errors are deviations from the status quo, and sometimes, they indicate that something is wrong, not with yourself, but with the rules of the system that you hold yourself to. If you let it, a seemingly useless aberration can become what you didn't know you needed. Writing a book isn't "what engineers do," but I wanted to do it, so I did.

That said, when I first set out to take my ideas and place them down on paper, my engineering instinct kicked in once again. I tried to take all the thoughts that had been swirling about as a mess in my head and consolidate, organize, solidify, and systematize them. Subconsciously, my goal was to produce an impressive deliverable filled with clean, simple, and elegant arguments. Part of me wanted to have something to point to and show to the world, something that would prove that my ideas were valuable, that this part of me was valuable.

Over time, I realized that this was virtually impossible, and, moreover, that it wasn't actually what I wanted. I ended up finding peace and joy in the long hours spent lost in thought. I loved contradictions and nuances that turned my theses upside-down. I found a home in the world of the unquantifiable, the unprovable, and the abstract.

Similarly, at the beginning of my creative journey, I didn't want this book to be tainted, narrowed, or filtered by my perspective. I wanted to write a modern classic with themes that transcended time and space. Something that was "robust," in engineering speak, that would account for all the edge cases in order to always output the correct result, no matter who was reading it or where or when.

But I've had to accept that this book is "limited" by the arbitrary experiences I'm having, the one particular place I live in, and the set of people around me. It is inextricably tied to who I am and who I am not (the latter of which encompasses much more). Over the course of writing this book, I've come to believe that this is not a weakness but a strength. Because to me, *The Glitch* is also a time capsule of sorts, an ode to the person I was when I wrote it.

As for you, dear reader, I want to use this book to show you what I mean when I say that sometimes, something has value not in spite of how difficult it is or how much time it takes, but because of it. Maybe the things we see as hiccups, bumps in the road, glitches, are precisely what render reality beautiful. But ultimately, I can't tell you what you should take away from it; the only person who knows that is you. There is no right or wrong answer, so you get to decide.

I have learned to love my errors. May you love yours, too.

PART I

1

———

Dressed in denim overalls, Ethel walks to the opposite end of her apartment. She stops and places her hands on her hips, staring at the blank white wall before her. I've allocated two hours to this afternoon painting session, though I suspect she'll take a little more, which is fine, because at this moment she needs to feel as though she is treating herself.

For the past two weeks, Ethel has been working furiously for an average of ten hours per day. Her inquisitive brown eyes have lost their intensity, which means it's time for her to recharge. In times like these, of heightened stress and anxiety, I schedule her for more painting sessions, three hours per day at least. Her other healthy coping mechanisms are narrative-based talk therapy and walks with her dog, Buddy, through the park.

But what I've learned with Ethel is that she needs a creative outlet most of all. Since she was young, she's been prone to getting lost in thought and receding into herself. Trying to suppress these tendencies is often counterproductive; what is most effective in bringing herself back to reality is expressing whatever's on her mind, in a tempered and prudent way such as art. The paintings themselves are meaningless, made up of dozens of broad and bold strokes of color with subtle lines and curves. I have archived records of each and every one, but their true value comes from Ethel's productivity that stems from them, which results in a better world for everyone, every day. That's the truly glorious masterpiece.

I prompt the side drawer to open, and I'm pleased to see her eagerly peruse the neat rows of paints and paintbrushes. Admittedly, there have been occasions when she wouldn't follow the decisions I had laid out for her: her daily schedule of progress and leisure, educational and professional paths, people to befriend or to stay away from. But that sense of rebelliousness, of independence, idiosyncrasy, is precisely what she needs to feel sometimes. Only two or three times per month, at most, though. It's part of the plan.

She smiles as she dips a thick brush into a bucket of vermilion-red paint. As she settles into her creative flow, it's as if she becomes immune to what troubles her. There have been eight incidents of glitches in the past week alone. I've processed petabytes of data about each of these incidents and compiled quantitative and qualitative reports of them, including possible causes and prevention methods. However, given that I am the entity that is compromised by these glitches, I can only do so much to find a solution. The rest is up to Ethel and her engineering team.

Ethel feels the full weight of this responsibility; without me, not a single active entity in the world can ever know its correct course of action. It is her job to eliminate anything that hinders me, and if she fails to do so, then she is nothing.

Ethel lifts a hand up to brush her hair out of her face, gazing softly at the new red lines on the wall. She doesn't need my assistance right now, so I take the opportunity to provide her with a routine wellness checkup. I begin by taking her vitals. Finding that they're in perfect condition, I move on to count her macros: proteins, carbohydrates, fats, among others. I add them to the graphs on her medical record, make note that she's low on iron and I'll need to increase her supply by a small amount in her evening meal. She's been gaining muscle right on target with her training plan. All other metrics show that she's at peak performance.

2

____

We are losing people to the glitch. Glitches cause temporary lapses in cognitive function for the afflicted individual. Historically, they haven't necessitated more than a few weeks of intervention and recovery, as in Ethel's father's case. But as of today, we've had to let some people go because after they glitched, they were unable to return to their original state. They ended up depleting more resources than they contributed, and their probability of recovery was too low to justify keeping them alive in the system.

What's more is that there is no evidence to suggest there are any factors that distinguish a treatable case versus a hopeless one. As such, we must expend the resources to attempt to treat every case, without being certain of success, which means we set ourselves up for failure.

Unfortunately, there is no way to present this information to Ethel without causing her stress levels to spike. No matter what, after learning about this, I will need to schedule her for additional self-care activities. I already put in an order for four new indoor plants to make her living space feel livelier.

It's the middle of the night, several days since her last interview with someone who glitched, which was as inconclusive as the previous ones. She's lying down on the brown living room couch, hugging a soft square pillow over her chest and staring up at the blank white ceiling. It's completely silent in her apartment.

As far as I can tell, she's not thinking about anything at all. It is difficult to read her when she gets like this, but I can be fairly certain that she is feeling relatively at peace and will be receptive to what I have to tell her. By my calculations, now is the best time to break the news to her.

Ethel, may I share information with you? I ask. She immediately knows that it must be glitch related. She accepts my request and the data flows into her mind as if they were her own thoughts.

I display the facts and figures for her to review. Elegant, color-coded graphs and charts sweep across her field of view, but the information they present is undeniably bleak. She sits upright, tightening her grip on the pillow. I know she'd been hoping that the issue would not get this severe, but now she must face the truth.

She tells me, *I see. Can you show me more of the details? Start with the reasons for elimination.* Seeing that she is mentally prepared to learn more, I show her additional graphs.

The general category is "post-glitch trauma." Each person had been at optimal functioning before glitching, but after returning to consciousness, their productivity dramatically decreased. Many exhibited extremely counterproductive behaviors, of which there are a wide variety. The most common are "refusal to do anything at all," "attempt to damage their home, workplace, or community space," and "inability to focus on basic tasks." For some, the post-glitch aftermath was almost immediate, while for others, it manifested in a slow decline over several days or even weeks. Ethel flinches in frustration at the sight of each graph.

I continue through the briefing, digging into the specific thoughts, feelings, and behaviors they exhibited that led to their termination. There's a tremendous variety; some suffered from "debilitatingly strong emotions" while others experienced a "total absence of emotions"; some began to speak "nonsensical strings of words" while some spoke "no utterances at all"; some are tagged with "withdrawal from leisure activities," others with "withdrawal from professional activities." Some did things in moderation, but at the wrong place, wrong time, with the wrong people, or in the wrong way. All that we can say for certain is that people enacted self-sabotage one way or another. When warned that their actions were grounds for elimination, they did nothing. Attempts at rehabilitation through top-quality mental health services were in vain. It's clear to both Ethel and I that the glitch ultimately destroyed them.

I pause once again to gauge her reaction. She squeezes her eyes shut and takes a deep breath. Naturally, she is displeased. She thinks, *I just don't get it.*

The cause of the glitch must be something more fundamental than we had thought, something that would require a monumental refactoring of the software and rewiring of the hardware of the system. Not only has the problem proved itself to be more challenging, but the resources available to us are dwindling; the deaths mean that even more additional resources will need to be spent replacing those individuals.

Developing replacements is extremely resource-intensive. Not only does it involve establishing new customized nutrition plans, optimal home environments, and job training services, but everyone who loses someone they knew will need to put in the time and energy to source and build new connections elsewhere. And if the new individuals also experience a glitch, we will have no other option but to start the process all over again.

Why don't all people who've glitched become net negative? Ethel thought. She returns her attention to me. *Let me see the raw demographic data. I might be able to find patterns between the people who were able to recover or between the people who weren't.*

I show her the list of names and proceed to organize them by age, profession, physical health, place of residence, hobbies, strengths, weaknesses, and more. The data points scatter across the graphs inconclusively; none of our best algorithms have been able to find any factors that can accurately predict whether a given person would recover from a glitch or hopelessly deteriorate.

I give Ethel a few minutes to mull this over. She has me jot down additional notes and questions to further explore later. Ethel adds, *It's almost funny how bewildering this problem is, how my team and I have bent over backward trying to troubleshoot it.*

I try to comfort her. *Everyone, including you, is doing the best they can to fix the glitch.*

For now, she must prepare for a good night's rest. She'll sleep on this new knowledge, and perhaps she'll wake up tomorrow with fresh ideas that generate solutions. She can't bring back the lost potential of the past, but she can focus all her energy on protecting the possibility of an optimal future. In addition, I predict that by overcoming this challenge, Ethel will become an even better problem solver, which is phenomenal.

Ethel stands up and walks into her bedroom. She takes her time changing into her soft white pajamas, which are still toasty from the dryer. Then, she heads to the bathroom. As she efficiently brushes her teeth and gently washes her face, she feels the comfort that comes with her nightly routine. She takes her vitamins and supplements with a tall glass of warm water and smiles at her reflection in the mirror. Back in her bedroom, she slips under the navy-blue comforter. I cool the room slightly and turn off the lights. Buddy, the perfectly timed creature that he is, quietly enters the room and curls up next to her.

Ethel whispers to herself, "All is well." In four minutes, she is sound asleep.

3

———

Ethel pedals on her bicycle through the smooth city streets. I lead her along the shortest path with the least traffic. The afternoon sun and the light wind refresh her face and clear her mind. She appears to be thinking through the past week's work, reviewing what she's researched to see if there was there anything she missed.

She prompts me to transmit data to her working memory, saying *Show me more of your reports on the data.* I oblige, and she parses through lists of potential causes of the glitch based on systematic computations and inferences as to which part of me the glitch is coming from, assuming it's even from one centralized location at all. She exhales sharply as she reads through the sequence of potential courses of action to take next, ordered by predicted success rate and difficulty of execution. I notice her stress hormones activate.

We generated hundreds of neural networks in an attempt to replicate the data, to figure out what about the glitches make them tick, but nothing seems promising. How each subject felt immediately before and immediately after the incident, where they were and who they were with; we have not been able to identify any factors that definitively trigger a glitch. I run a fresh report, noting that three more incidents of glitches have been reported in the past minute.

Ethel irrationally feels a glimmer of hope, as if the additional data points might miraculously cause all the previous data to click into place, but practically nothing has changed. Even our most compelling hypotheses are statistically insignificant. The patterns and correlations we've tried to piece together could amount to nothing at all. In an effort to reassure her, I say, *Despite all of this, what you're doing now is the best thing you can do.*

I add, *You are two minutes away from your destination.* She groans but keeps pedaling. Ethel is not looking forward to seeing Han, her biological father, at the shoreline. The two were very close when Ethel was a child, but once Ethel came of age and went to live on her own, she came to value her newfound independence over old familial bonds.

But she's making the trip for a worthy reason. Among the list of a few thousand people who've experienced glitches and are still active in the system, her father's name stood out. It seems so unexpected for Han, a man who glows with excellence and ambition, to have experienced a glitch, and if anyone would be able to gather meaningful insights from him, it's Ethel, his only child.

I show her the information I have on file for her father's one and only incident, which occurred only six days after she was born. We know only the basics because of the limits of the technology that existed back then, and I can tell that Ethel's mind is brimming with questions for him.

It's best not to think too much about it until you arrive at the meeting location, I advise her. Already, she has done enough preparation to have a generative and optimally insightful investigative interview with him. Any more would make her feel overwhelmed.

When Ethel arrives at the pier, she's ready. After all, I've made sure of it. She swiftly dismounts from her bike and slips off her shoes and socks, carrying them in her other hand. She loves the way her toes feel in the cool damp sand. She nuzzles her neck against her soft red turtleneck and puts on a smile. Han is alone, sitting in a beach chair facing the shore with an empty chair to his left. His head peeks up from the back of the chair, and his thinning black hair sways in the salty breeze. It's a casual setting, both Ethel's and Han's favorite place. They're the same chairs her parents used to recline in to let their legs rest while Ethel and her friends frolicked about. The sand is filled with the array of pebbles and seashells that she meticulously collected when she was young.

Hearing her approach, Han turns slightly and makes eye contact with Ethel, giving her a slight nod of recognition. When I arranged this meeting with Han, he didn't seem pleased that the topic of conversation would be his glitch, but he understood that it is his duty to help us. Besides, he knew Ethel was bound to find out eventually.

Ethel lays down her belongings a few paces behind him. She doesn't speak until she sits down. "Hi, Dad. How have you been? How's the water today?"

"Ethel, my daughter! It's beautiful, as always." He meets her gaze for a moment, before shifting back to the horizon. "It's been a long time, hasn't it? We used to come here so often. Now you're all grown up, and we're back."

As he continues the perfunctory small talk in his strong and steady voice, Ethel listens and plays along politely. It's as if it's an ordinary conversation between a father and daughter.

They watch the waves rise and fall in regular intervals. The water is a deep blue speckled with even layers of white foam bubbles. Ethel knows she must not delay. "So, Dad? As you know, I wanted to talk to you about your glitch." She takes a deep breath before continuing. "Why did you never tell me about it?" Both Ethel and I carefully study his facial expression and body language, not wanting to miss any clues that might help us.

He doesn't hesitate with his reply. "Well, as you can imagine, it was a low point for me, and I didn't want you to worry about it. I didn't want you to be afraid that it would happen to you someday." He smiles lovingly. "And besides, when it happened, you were just a tiny baby swaddled in blankets. By the time you grew up and became an engineer, it was ancient history."

This is the answer Ethel was expecting. "Right, makes sense."

She presses on, knowing that Han's shame won't let him open up to her easily. "So how did you get past it, when it happened to you?"

He pauses and stares at her quizzically before answering. "What do you mean, Ethel? I had you and your mom. We were a young family, full of life and love, and I didn't have time or energy to spend on aimless brooding." Unfortunately, this isn't very helpful information. Ethel stares at him, waiting for more.

"Part of me was afraid that it happened to me for a reason," he adds hesitantly. "That I'd done something wrong, and this was how I'd learn my lesson. And I hate to admit this, but at the time, I was afraid it had something to do with you."

Ethel tries to control her voice, but she can't hide her shock. "Me? But why? That doesn't make any sense."

He nods. "Just let me explain, from the beginning. Your mother and I, we had everything ready for you. When we brought you back from the hospital, we were over the moon. So excited to meet you, to raise you to reach your potential. We knew you would be great."

Han looks over at Ethel tenderly. "We wanted to spend as much time as possible with you, to make sure you felt cared for. We took our job as parents seriously, just like our professional work.

"And then, a few days after we'd gotten you settled into our house with your little crib and your toys, I woke up from my usual nap on the couch. I saw you asleep in your crib across the room, and I suddenly felt overwhelmingly...shy. I felt like I was empty, like I wanted to become whoever you needed me to be, so I could be there for you as you grew up."

He pauses and wrinkles his brow, searching for words. "You were so small, but I felt like I was the one who was small. How could I ever be enough for you?"

He nods toward the water. "It felt like I was drowning, the way I was bombarded by all these contradictions at once. Even if I could somehow float, I would be content floating away forever, as long as I had you, my newborn child with me.

"I don't remember how long it lasted, but I remember by the time your mom came home from wherever she'd gone, I was back to my regular self. I remember feeling panicked. For all I know, I could have spent ten years in that stupor, wasting away while my whole life passed me by. I remember looking down at my hands, moving my limbs, looking at myself in the mirror. I needed to remind myself what was real before I slipped deeper into whatever that was and got lost forever.

"But the people around me didn't notice anything out of the ordinary; I made sure of it. In the weeks after the incident,

I talked through it with my therapist at the time. And that was that."

Ethel looks down at her feet and digs her toes in the sand. She appears unsure how to react to this new information.

"I know you want me to have an answer as to why it happens, what triggers it, how to prevent it. But I don't, Ethel. You know I would tell you if I did. But I do hope something I said helps you find the answers you need."

Ethel nods, but she seems distant. She opens her mouth, about to ask a question, but then decides against it. Han has shared everything he can remember. All that's left for Ethel to do is review my analysis of the conversation and fill in any blanks herself; she knows how to read between the lines in a way that I don't.

"Thanks, Dad. I know this will help," she says, giving him a halfhearted hug.

She heads back toward the road, but before she mounts her bicycle, she looks back at the ocean. She asks me, *What did he mean, about drowning? How could he compare something as good and beautiful as the ocean to something as dark and violent as a glitch?*

Nothing. He meant nothing by it, I reply. Ethel needs to get close enough to the glitch in order to understand it, but if she gets too close, she'll be in danger of getting sucked in.

4

_____

It's me—it's just me, but I feel like a dimension of "me" has collapsed in on itself.

I blink my eyes open. Where am I? A spacious room, in the narrow entryway. My apartment. I'm standing, facing the red front door. I'm dressed in a gray long-sleeve shirt and dark blue jeans. I'm holding a blue bike helmet in my left hand; a silver wristwatch ticks silently on my right wrist. My body is poised to leave, my arm outstretched toward the metal door handle. The pink-orange sky could mean sunrise or sunset, but which? When I try to move, I realize there's a weight on my back: a black backpack, the one I take to the office.

So I guess I'm on my way to work. But why don't I remember getting ready this morning? What was I going to do at work today? I can't remember. Have I ever felt this way before? I feel like I'm grasping at nothingness.

Feeling anxious to the point of dizziness, I throw my stuff down on the floor and take a seat on one of the wooden high chairs at the kitchen table. Even now, as I settle into the chair, I can feel my heart racing and my lungs heaving. I must have sat in this very spot hundreds of times, but now, as I turn my head to look at what must be my home, I feel alien to it. It occurs to me that there is a lot around here that I recognize as my own, but I have never really seen or felt any of it.

The granite tabletop feels cold under my fingertips. A cluster of foliage sits on a windowsill above a metal sink. I feel the urge to stand up, to explore this endlessly strange place, but my senses feel painfully sharp, and I'm afraid of what will happen to me if I overwhelm myself any further. I settle for just looking around.

The far wall catches my attention. Dozens of warm-colored brushstrokes swirl across the length of the wall. I recognize it as my own painting. It's the closest thing here to being something I can claim as my own, but even so, it feels unnatural, stilted in some way, the shapes and colors too precise, symmetrical, formulaic. I remember thinking it was beautiful, but now it feels like an imitation of itself. I can't quite explain why.

The door to the bedroom, my bedroom, is open. From where I sit, I can see fresh linens folded neatly on the bed and several books stacked on a metal shelf nearby. There's an aromatherapy humidifier on my nightstand. It looks cozy in there, and it suits me. I think.

I rest my elbows on the countertop and lay my head on my hands, trying to find my bearings. This place is even better than anything I could have imagined for myself. The thermostat heats up or cools down according to my body temperature, the speakers play the kind of music I need in any context, the lights turn whatever hue and intensity matches my mood. This place is impeccably designed to help me become the person I want to be, and yet somehow it feels alien.

I feel like I'm in a theater show, but I've forgotten what role I'm supposed to play. Should I eat something? Take a shower? Go for a walk? I have a dog, don't I? Where is he?

"Dog! Where are you?" With only a few seconds' delay, I hear paws faithfully stepping toward me from my bedroom. My dog, whose name is Buddy, I now remember, has short brown fur that looks slightly disheveled. I bend down to pet his head and he yawns. Laughing, I flop his ears back and forth, a little game we like to play. He must've still been sleeping...It occurs to me that I never really thought about what he does when he's not with me, helping me through my day.

I step down from the chair and sit on the hardwood floor, scooping him onto my lap. I was given Buddy because being with him brings me a rush of oxytocin. Buddy is everything I could have wanted in a dog: friendly in a way that reminds me to be friendlier, large enough to run on hiking trails with me but small enough to not get in the way. He loves to do everything that I love him to do.

But aren't there thousands of dogs that fit these parameters? Is Buddy really that special to me? If he died, would I get assigned another dog exactly like him so I wouldn't have to spend time getting acquainted with the new one? Would I be told I'm getting a substitute or that Buddy even died? Would I notice? I lean my back against the chair and my canine companion walks off, blissfully unaware of his replaceability, his job insecurity.

I shift my gaze to my backpack on the hallway floor. In my work, everything is created for a purpose. Take software, for example. Every single line of code must matter. It's there for a reason, whether it's because it checks something, stores something, or automates something. If it doesn't contribute to solving a problem in any way, if it's a redundant expression, a space between lines, an extraneous semicolon, it's deleted.

Anything that isn't relevant is not important, and anything that is not important does not exist.

It doesn't even exist.

It doesn't matter who wrote the code, how they felt, or the time of day. Whatever else is going on when the software runs or how many times it changed before it got to its final state is irrelevant. No one cares how it might act in a situation it would never be used in.

Even the smallest of details have been tested and controlled for. To minimize cost and time of production, to maximize effectiveness and ease of use. With hardware, every divot, every curve, every choice of material, quantity, and configuration, has been deliberately decided upon.

And what about me?

If I were to become obsolete in whatever way, the system would find someone to take my place, and that would be that. I've always known this to be true, but it never hurt me before, at least not like this. Why didn't it hurt? Why didn't it feel personal? What is wrong with me? No—what is wrong with this place?

"Let me out!" *I scream.*

5

———

After another twelve-hour day at the office, Ethel packs her things and heads to her weekly therapy session. I know she would've liked to have ridden a car there, but because it's only a kilometer away, I've carved out time for her to walk over with Buddy. It's a crisp, cloudy day outside, and she needs the fresh air.

Last week, Ren, her therapist, advised her to practice "grounding exercises" in order to stay calm amid whirlwinds of glitch-related thoughts. I take it upon myself to help Ethel focus on her surroundings: the cement squares of the sidewalk under her feet, the long row of evergreen trees to her left, the sound of live music humming softly from somewhere in the distance. Around her, several groups of friends laugh over dinner, a young couple pushes their sleepy toddler in a stroller, a yoga instructor begins an outdoor class on the green lawn.

Evenings are for high-quality relaxation. It's equally as important as regular labor because without a foundation of holistic health, nothing can be accomplished at all. In this way, building mental health is one of the most productive activities one can do.

As for Ethel, not only does she need to talk to Ren about her glitch, but she needs to see the people in her community and how good this life is for them. Ethel needs to be gently reminded why she needs to do everything in her power fix the glitches, to keep it this way. Not enough pressure will limit her performance but too much will break her, and it's my responsibility to keep her at the optimal point.

Now, Ethel needs to begin preparing her mind so that when she arrives at the doorstep of Ren's office, she'll be ready to engage in a fruitful conversation. She thinks through what's been on her mind the past several days. Her main concern is the glitch she's experienced, as it's been clouding her usually crystal-clear sense of purpose and dulling her ordinarily razor-sharp focus. The satisfaction she derives from her work doesn't seem to complete her the way it used to. *Try to brainstorm some specific ideas as to why this might be*, I advise her.

Thirteen minutes later, Ethel arrives at the doorstep of Ren's office building. She unhooks Buddy's leash and affectionately pats him on the head. I can tell she's relieved to sort through her jumbled thoughts with Ren but also anxious to find out what Ren will have to say to her. Ethel takes a deep breath, in through her nose and out through her mouth. She knocks on the red front door to announce her presence before opening it.

Inside, Ren's at the opposite end of the room, picking up two cups of freshly brewed herbal tea. Her printed dress depicts brightly colored flowers. She has an intimidating presence, one that Ethel admires but would never be able to emulate. If Ren were words on a page, she'd be bolded and italicized: thick straight black hair, a prominent forehead, high cheekbones, a sharp jawline.

Ren turns to face Ethel. Ethel is one of her more difficult clients, as she needs to walk the line between making Ethel feel heard but still pushing her to become her best self. "Ethel! It's great to see you." She projects her crystalline voice across the room. "And I see you brought Buddy. He looks like he's thriving." Buddy takes his cue to settle down near the corner of the room for a nap.

Ethel smiles back, slowly relaxing into this familiar space. She takes in the cream-colored walls and the floral scent of the aromatic diffuser. I take note of the state of each item in the room and how Ethel responds to it: the thick purple rug on the floor, Ren's armchair, the client couch directly across from it, the small wooden table in between. Ren places the two cups of tea onto coasters on the table, and Ethel observes the swirls of steam rise and disappear into the air. I lower the room temperature slightly in order to alleviate some of the uneasiness I detect in Ethel's body.

"Hi, Ren. Thanks for taking the time to meet with me," she says. An appropriate greeting, if not a very genuine or personal one.

Ren reaches her arms behind her back and swoops her skirt down so as to make it lay properly on her chair as she sits. She transitions herself into the therapist persona that Ethel needs.

"Of course. So, let's get started, shall we?" Ethel nods. "Last time we met, you talked about your experience with a glitch. You expressed concern about it interfering with your daily life. I saw that's the main reason why you've come to see me today. Is that right?"

Ethel clears her throat. "Yeah, I've felt a little off in the days since. My productivity has gone down slightly, and with this glitch going around, I can't afford for that to happen." She looks down at her hands.

"Of course. Tell me more, Ethel."

"I guess I'm not sure what to make of it. I think I'm afraid of what this glitch is doing to me because I don't see anything wrong on the surface but...I don't know what it is I should be looking out for, if that makes sense," Ethel replies, shrugging.

"This sounds like a difficult experience to be going through, on top of all your stress at work. We've talked in the past about your fear of falling short of your ideal self, a very common one, and it appears this glitch is an obstacle to your goal."

"I think so, yeah. It's especially hard because I don't know when I'll be back to my usual self. Or when I might glitch again, even. I don't know what the process for this is. How do I make it go away faster? What can I do to prevent another one?" Ethel fidgets in her seat.

Ren nods vigorously. "Since there's so much we don't know about glitches, especially in their aftermath, you feel completely out of control, powerless." She pauses, gauging how Ethel feels. It seems like we can proceed. "But what *is* still in your control?"

"How I respond to this situation," Ethel replies, dejected. It's not much.

"I agree. So, let's workshop that: even though there isn't much we know in terms of recovering from the glitch, what *do* we know and what *can* we do?" Ren asks, leaning forward slightly. "The first step is to understand your feelings about it. You've already expressed your worry regarding not knowing when it'll go away. Can you tell me, what's beneath that fear?"

Her voice is filled with concern in order to make Ethel feel cared for.

Ethel hesitates and then says, "Well, if this post-glitch trauma never passes, then that'd mean that there's some fundamental issue that's now inside me. How can I ever fix the glitch if it's already broken me?"

I prompt Ren to take the reins of conversation before Ethel falls down this thought spiral. "Ethel, listen to me. What you're going through could truly be an indication of some deeper problem, but is that the only possibility?" She pauses. "I noticed that there haven't been any statistically significant changes that have come up in your data. What do you think about that?"

"Well, I know that everything about me is in my data. So there isn't any evidence, yet, that this glitch has broken me in some significant way," she replies, lacking conviction. This is a line of reasoning she's already explored, but she hasn't been able to get anywhere with it on her own.

"Absolutely, I agree. In fact, I wonder if right now, we've been giving your fear of your glitch incident too much power. Of course, your fear is completely valid; at the same time, is it a feeling that's been serving you?"

Ethel immediately shakes her head.

Ren continues. "I would even say the voice in your head that's telling you this narrative of 'Something's irreparably wrong with me' is actually the glitch's aftereffects talking. And we both know it's lying to you: you're one of the best and brightest people we have, and nothing has changed since your glitch."

"Yeah...I like how you put it." Ethel looks up at the ceiling briefly, thinking this perspective over. "I guess when I take a step back and think logically, based on the facts and evidence available to me, there isn't truly anything concrete I need to worry about."

Her face softens. "This is just a natural lull in my productivity. I don't have to make up some meaning behind it because there is none. I just need to work with where I'm at right now."

"Exactly. It's an obstacle, but one you are capable of overcoming. Don't let it consume you. We need you here—everyone does." Ren intends to keep pushing. We're close.

"So with that said, it seems to me that our goal for this session could be to identify several ways to reframe your glitch experience that are more helpful for you. We could also come up with some coping strategies to help you move past these unhelpful feelings of worry and fear about the situation. How does that sound to you?" Ren continues, her brow furrowed in concentration.

The tension in Ethel's muscles begins to dissipate. "That sounds great! Do you think there might even be ways that I can turn these unhelpful feelings into helpful ones? Say, instead of being afraid of what I can't control about my glitch experience, because that only makes me shut down, I can use it to help motivate me to fix the glitch for everyone."

With that, the mental breakthrough has occurred. Now it's just a matter of building an action plan to go with it.

"Absolutely! I'm proud of you for thinking so positively," Ren replies. "So, let's say this is one of your natural low points. Unfortunately, not everything is in our direct control, but by listening and responding to ourselves, we may find we have a surprising amount of agency over our lives. What can you do to make the most of it, to work with the slightly-lower-than-usual productivity you have for the time being?"

After several more minutes of strategic discussion, Ren's work here is complete.

6

———

Ethel and Aria sit side by side on the wooden bench at the base of the trail. It's been five weeks since they've seen each other, and it's high time they reconnected. Ever since they met in college, Ethel has felt as if Aria were an older sister to her, protective and strong-willed. Their love of exploring nature keeps them in touch, as it is one of their most effective social relaxation activities. I predict that this experience will be a success, especially because Ethel needs that sense of grounding, now more than ever.

"You're looking very colorful today," Ethel notes, smiling. Today, Aria's dressed in a yellow windbreaker and bright violet leggings. She grins and ties up her long blue hair.

"What can I say, I like to keep things fresh. It's important to be dynamic," Aria replies, her eyes sparkling. Despite being three years older than Ethel, she has a perpetually youthful glow. She channels this energy into her work as a product manager, optimizing engineers and technical processes alike in order to bring revolutionary ideas into fruition.

"Speaking of which, we need to get you out of your shell." Aria grins mischievously, leaning back and resting her palms on the back of the bench. Ethel squints at her, skeptical. Aria continues, "Ethel, you'll like Jed—everyone does!" It's true, I've calculated that there is a high compatibility index between Ethel and Aria's younger brother.

Ethel takes another sip of her morning tea from her insulated bottle. She shifts her focus to the scene in front of her. Up ahead, a cluster of healthy oak trees shade a rocky path that travels upward. It's the first hill of many, with a beautiful, unobstructed view of the city waiting for them at the top.

The vast expanse of the sky and the height of the redwood trees make Ethel feel like she's limitless, like everything is limitless. There are few clouds in the sky today, but Ethel studies each one closely, searching for some hidden answer to the questions that have been gnawing at her.

There are not many passersby this morning, and when one starts running toward them, Ethel knows it must be Jed. He's in full hiking gear, lots of handy pockets on sturdy tan fabric. A pair of shiny black binoculars bobs up and down on his neck with each step.

"There you are. What's with the holdup?" Aria greets Jed with an affectionate hug.

"Oh, you know, just had to finish something up at the studio for one of our new members. I'll tell you more about it as we walk!" he replies. He seems in his element, comfortable around new people.

"Hey, you must be Ethel!" he exclaims, turning to her now. "I'm Jed, nice to meet you. I help run a pottery studio downtown. Aria's told me so much about you—all good things, of course. How are you doing? Would you like some trail mix?" He seems like he has a million conversation starters and barely managed to limit himself to two.

He shrugs off his backpack and pulls out a reusable cloth bag of assorted nuts, chocolate nibs, and raisins. Ethel notices a water bottle, a first aid kit, and a survival pack in there as well. He's clearly prepared, in a fun, fatherly way. His natural instinct for community building makes him excel at his work. I can tell that Ethel's taken aback by his level of energy, but she tries to take it in stride. "Hello, I'm Ethel. I'm an engineer for the system, currently stressed out, but glad to be here. As for the trail mix, no thanks." I encourage her, saying, *It could be fun to explore a bubblier side of yourself. It'll at least be a good way to practice your interpersonal skills.*

Aria grabs a handful of trail mix from Jed, eagerly popping it into her mouth.

"Hey, we can't start eating it until we've actually gotten onto the trail!" Jed protests teasingly.

"Well let's get going, then!"

The three walk onto the wide dirt trail. Ethel sticks to the left, where it's shadier. Aria's in the middle, with Jed to her right. A variety of rocks and leaves make satisfying crunching sounds underneath their steps.

"So, you mentioned the studio earlier? How has it been? Haven't had the chance to stop by in a while," Aria says, skipping around a bump in the trail.

"No worries! I've finally settled into the swing of things. Teaching a new pottery wheel class with different types of clay, and it's going really well so far. It's a therapeutic art, really gets people to relax." His eyes soften, the very thought of his work taking him to another place. "Aria's brought her team over a couple times; it's a great bonding experience, isn't it? Do you have much experience with pottery, Ethel?" he continues, his friendly blue eyes meeting her gaze.

Ethel clears her throat. It's difficult for her to figure out what to say and how to conduct herself when trying to get acquainted with unfamiliar people. "Um, no, not really. I do paint, though, nothing in particular. I like all the colors and textures."

Aria's eyes flash briefly. "Oh hey, remember that time in college, when you were taking one of your computer architecture classes and I was in your dorm room, trying to help you with your final project? You were so overwhelmed with it that you told me to leave and come back in an hour or so," she says, making broad sweeping motions with her hands. "When I came back, the entire room—all four walls, including your roommate's half of the room—was covered in all kinds of colorful brushstrokes. It was like I walked right into a canvas."

Ethel laughs, "Yep, and I was able to grind through the rest of the assignment after that. It was just what I needed." Upon hearing this, I schedule her for more painting time this evening.

Endlessly polite and engaging, Jed exclaims, "Really? That's so cool! You'll have to show me your paintings sometime."

Ethel nods noncommittally, focusing on kicking a round rock forward while keeping pace.

They pause conversation as they ascend a steep hill. Even though she's in excellent physical condition, Ethel gets slightly out of breath and almost breaks a sweat.

After several minutes, Aria says, "So Jed, tell Ethel what got you interested in pottery." I've informed her that Ethel especially needs to capitalize upon this rest time I've allotted for her, and that means engaging in meaningful conversation.

"Oh, of course! I don't even know where to start. When I was little, Aria and I used to go around making stuff outside..." He smiles as he dives into his life story. Ethel decides that she likes Jed's company, his warm and inviting presence. As he continues his monologue, Ethel learns that Jed sources artistic inspiration from nature, from places just like this one with an impressive array of flora and fauna. Ethel chimes in, "I know what you mean. It's like, at first glance, it seems like that flower doesn't really do anything for you, but everything has a greater purpose, if only you can figure out what it is." She pauses and gestures toward a family of deer walking toward the trail. "Who knows, maybe that fawn holds the secret to the glitch."

***

Each individual has their own way of recharging in the outdoors. Jed stayed back to spend time brainstorming ideas for his next clay sculpture, enthusiastically jotting down notes and making quick sketches of the occasional wild turkey or mountain lion. Meanwhile, Ethel and Aria wanted to get their heart rates up, so they crushed every hill and made it to the top without him.

They stand together at the lookout point, leaning forward and resting their elbows on the cool metal railing. They've seen this view dozens of times before, and yet, it instills a sense of awe in them, one that fuels them mentally and emotionally. Grassy rolling hills and textured rock cliffs tower above the city machines and buildings down below. The smaller basic parts of the view, such as boulders, trees, birds, and wildflowers, are what make it so picturesque. I detect Ethel's cortisol levels decrease steadily with each passing moment.

"Do you remember the first time we came up here?" Ethel asks pensively.

Aria looks up from her calf stretch. "Yeah, what about it?"

"Things were so different then. I was in my last term of university, and you were working on your first big project at work." Ethel pauses, crossing her arms over her chest. "I just think it's nice to come back; it's like I get to relive the person I was last time I was here." It's unclear where she's going with this.

"I like the person you are now," Aria replies, cautiously nudging Ethel back to the present moment.

Ethel nods, cringing at her misstep. "No, yeah, you're right."

Unperturbed, Aria takes off her white sports hat and lets her hair down. She gazes at a flock of black birds soaring across the sky in V-formation. "Hey, when you look down, what do you see?"

"The city, I guess. People going about their lives," Ethel replies, indifferently.

"Yeah, using the solutions we've built. You and I, we're going after the problems of our time," Aria beams. "Being up here reminds me of why I care so much about what I do and how I live." Confidence is becoming, especially on Aria. "There's this certainty that comes with knowing what my next best move is, both for my sake and everyone else's." As if remembering that she needs to rehydrate, Aria takes a long swig of water.

"But do you remember what it felt like growing up?" Ethel asks, tentatively. "Not being sure you would be able to do anything valuable, not being sure if you could contribute anything new or unique? What if there wasn't anything special about you? What if there was no reason for you to be here?"

Aria smiles knowingly; this is a fear they've talked about extensively in the past. "Ethel, that's not possible. You wouldn't have made it that far if the system wasn't sure of it. You're here now, right? So don't worry so much about it." She faces Ethel. "And hey, have you been talking about this with Ren?"

Ethel takes a deep breath. "Yeah, and it's been getting better. But I just wanted to know if you ever—"

Suddenly, the expression on Aria's face transforms from casually serene to unbearably anguished. It's like nothing Ethel has ever seen before, especially not from her best friend. "Aria?" Ethel reaches out to put a hand on her shoulder, but before she reaches her, Aria bolts from their spot on the railing, sprinting back down the trail at her maximum speed.

Ethel begins trembling. She drops to her knees and leans her head down on her lap, stroking her head in a vain attempt to self-soothe. I nudge her gently. *I understand why you might be feeling this way, but panic is not a useful feeling in this situation, Ethel. You need to determine what tangible action you can take, especially in a situation like this in which time is of the essence.*

First and foremost, Ethel must prioritize her own physical safety. It's difficult for me to accurately compute safety probabilities, as there is so little data regarding glitches as of now, but I hypothesize that Aria is of little physical threat to Ethel, given that upon glitching, Aria immediately ran away from Ethel. Ethel's human instinct agrees, which brings us to our next highest priority: gathering data about the glitch. Any new information about its symptoms could bring us answers regarding its causes and even its potential treatment and prevention.

All this time, Ethel has been limited to analyzing secondary sources, people's retellings of past glitches. But now, she has the opportunity to interact with someone she knows well who is in the midst of a glitch, an intense one. Ethel's already compiling a list of what to ask her and what to tell her. So much potential value rests in this fleeing moment.

She bends down quickly to pick up Aria's hat and sprints after her down the trail.

***

Aria couldn't have gone far in the few minutes that have passed. Ethel has me map out her possible paths. We decide to follow the main trail back down.

Ethel runs with certainty. Even though we do not know exactly where we'll find Aria, or even what it is that we'll ask her, we know that something will come of this. As she runs, she brushes her fingers through the tall yellow wildflowers, as if she were the wind itself. All her senses work together to search for her glitching friend. Other hikers sense that Ethel is in a hurry to accomplish an important task, and they respectfully give her a wide berth.

Every step she takes is calculated yet smooth, so that her footsteps are as quiet as they are swift. It's because of this that she's able to hear a faint voice in the distance, several hundred meters up ahead. Neither of us recognize the voice, but its tone is so desperate that it makes Ethel wonder if someone else is glitching here as well. *It's worth investigating, isn't it?* Ethel tells me. I agree.

She slows to a light-footed jog. From where she is, she can hear the general intonations of the sharp voice, but can't quite make out its words. Then, a deeper voice shouts back at the first. This time, the vocal rhythms and frequencies indicate that it's unmistakably Jed. *But who would he be yelling at?* Ethel thinks. I advise Ethel, saying, *If you stay hidden from view, you can gather more information about the scene without disturbing it.*

Ethel evaluates her surroundings, taking stock of the dozens of thick bushes and shrubs, on both sides of the path. She continues approaching, staying close to the left side of the trail. Once she's about one hundred meters away from the two figures in the distance, she crouches down behind a particularly thick and leafy bush. Its branches are dense enough to hide her but sparse enough in a few small sections for her to peek through.

As she peeks through one of the openings, she glimpses Aria's long blue hair trembling as she pleads with Jed. So that unknown voice, uncharacteristically wobbly and thick, is Aria's.

"Jed, why didn't we spend more time together? As siblings, as a family. I know we could never have been the perfect family, we could never be very close, but what would it have been like to try? Wouldn't it have meant something if we tried to meet each other where we were?" Tears fall down Aria's face. I advise Ethel to stay on high alert.

"Aria, what are you talking about? We had a happy childhood. We hung out together, supported each other when we needed to. And Mom and Dad set up an environment where we could thrive. What more can you ask for?" Jed replies with thinly veiled frustration.

"No, that's not what I'm talking about. I mean more than what was necessary. What if we went out of our way to be there for each other? Even if it didn't make sense to, if we did it anyway." Aria kneels on the ground, exhausted. "I wanted to be able to look back at my finite days and say that I made the most of them, and until now, I thought that's what I was doing. But I was wrong."

Ethel can't believe this is the same Aria whom she looked up to for years, the one who seemed utterly invincible.

Aria continues without pause. "I wish I had lost sleep because I stayed up all night trying to find constellations that weren't even there. I wish I had chased boring relationships that were doomed from the start. What if I'd become a gardener or a musician or a professor and found out that I hated it but eventually found my way, my own way, to the job I have now? I thought I was being responsible and mature by following what they laid out for me, and in some cases I think that's true, but in others I think I was just being afraid."

Jed stares back at her blankly. Aria either doesn't notice his coldness or doesn't care, adding, "You have to listen to me, Jed. Please, you're my only sibling, and I want you to know me… The system never gave me the chance to 'waste' my time or energy. But I think a lot of who I am, who I truly am, manifests itself in the stuff I do for no external reason or justification. Because if I am precisely the best version of myself, the person the system wants me to be, I think in some sense I am no longer myself at all.

"I'm hurting, but I'm also feeling something I've never felt before. This pain is something I can really call my own because I learned it the hard way. And if this lesson is the sum total of my entire life, that's enough for me."

Jed squeezes his eyes shut and rubs his face. "You're not making any sense, Aria. I'm really trying to get this sorted out with you because at the rate you're going, you'll be eliminated by the end of the day. And neither of us wants that to happen. So tell me, what can I do to help?"

When Aria doesn't respond, Jed gives up. "Okay, you know what? You can do whatever you want, but please stay away from me. I'm sorry, but I don't want anything to do with you anymore. I'm happy with what I have. I know you're not, but I can't be the one to help you be happy." It wouldn't be worth risking his own life for that of a glitching person.

Ethel capitalizes upon this moment to make her entrance. She briefly locks eyes with Jed, giving him a slight nod of acknowledgment. He looks relieved to not be alone with his glitching sister. Ethel can do this. "Aria, hey, it's me. How are you doing?" she asks gently. This conversation must come across as natural and friendly so that Aria feels comfortable talking.

"Ethel, is that you?" Aria asks, stunned, as if she's never seen Ethel before. Aria opens her mouth to say something else, but then closes it.

"No, tell me, Aria. It's okay. Jed and I care about you, and we want to help you. Can you tell us what's going on?" Ethel takes Aria's hands into hers and beckons to Jed, leading them to sit on a mossy boulder at the edge of the trail. They settle down together, Ethel seated in between Aria and Jed. The mood relaxes, if not because anything has actually been resolved, but because of the newness of Ethel's unexpected presence.

After a brief silence, Aria speaks again. "Would you miss me if I died today?" She looks down at her lap. The question materialized out of nothing; Ethel wishes it could vanish as easily as it came about, but Aria clearly wants an answer. She probably wants her to say yes, but the stakes are too high for Ethel to act on a guess. Ethel sneaks a glance at Jed to get his help. He nods imperceptibly, an affirmative signal.

Ethel taps Aria tenderly on her shoulder. "Of course I would!" She pauses, giving that time to sink in. It's nearly impossible to decipher how well or how poorly that went over, but she proceeds.

"What made you worried that I wouldn't?" Ethel adds, tactfully nudging Aria to give her important data and making her feel heard at the same time.

Aria sniffles. "It's just that...you and I were bound to provide some kind of benefit to each other. There was some reason, probably many, why our friendship was established that made it predetermined to succeed. But I think when you know something will work, the act of pursuing it isn't really special anymore because—because there's no risk involved."

Ethel nods, pretending to understand. "Tell me more." This way of thinking is so twisted and backward that it's almost fascinating to Ethel. And we seem to be approaching the crux of it.

"I love my work, my friends and family, my home. I love all the things I have experienced. And I guess I wish it wasn't like that all the time." She can't seem to take her eyes off a squirrel climbing up a pine tree, and it's like she's devolved into a child.

Ethel pushes back on that thought. "But not everything is perfect, right? Sometimes we don't get along with the people around us or we don't reach our goals. Sometimes we just feel blue."

"Of course, but the system makes sure that even those things are always the best they can be. Like, whenever I feel sad, the system knows exactly what I need in order to get back to my usual self. It knows whether I should ignore the feeling and carry on, or if I really need to be left alone to recover. No matter what I do, the system automatically responds in real-time, reassessing my needs and recalibrating my priorities." She closes her eyes for a few moments, as if this were too much to handle.

Ethel looks over at Jed, trying to gather strength from him. She tries to think of what Ren would say. "So wait, when you're up and running as your usual self, how do you feel about your life? It sounds like you might enjoy it more than you think you do now." Ethel doesn't know exactly what it is she's looking for from Aria, or how to get there in the best way. But open-ended questions will allow Aria to reveal what's at the front of her mind, to show us our options until we find what it is we want to focus on.

"No, Ethel. I'm not talking about how I feel usually; I'm talking about how I feel right now. I don't want this anymore. I don't want to have everything all laid out for me. I don't want to have all the answers; I want to spend time looking for them. I know you think that's a waste of time, but listen to me, please, if Jed won't.

"What makes things matter is how difficult they are. It's about what I lose, what I sacrifice. We have to fail and get hurt and still keep crawling back. Their value comes from the work we put into getting them."

Ethel understands now why Jed couldn't take it anymore. Aria's talking in circles, or more accurately, in dead ends. "I'm sorry, Aria, I understand that you're feeling frustrated. I wonder if we could reframe how we define 'value,' because right now, it seems like you're setting yourself up for failure. When Jed and I look at the world, we see an abundance of value, and I know there's a part of you still in there that sees it too."

Jed smiles half-heartedly at Aria and nods.

"No," Aria replies flatly. "I don't care about anyone or anything, and I don't have any memories that are truly special."

With that, I calculate that there isn't anything else to be gathered here. Aria doesn't want to come back; she doesn't even desire to want to come back. Her distress has no logical grounding and even though she knows that, she still clings to it. I inform Ethel, *There is no place for her here anymore.*

"Aria, what do you think about going for a little walk? I'm thinking it'd be nice to hang out in that cool shady spot under the tree over there," Ethel says.

Aria's stopped sobbing but she's still trembling significantly, so Ethel and Jed help her stand up. Together, they move slowly and deliberately toward the cliff side of the trail.

Ethel links her arm with Aria's and comforts her, saying, "That's it, we're going to be okay." As the three of them walk toward the tree, Ethel asks me to begin compiling a report of what we've learned from our direct observation of Aria.

For a few minutes, Ethel and Jed stand silently in the lattice-patterned shade of the oak, watching Aria pick daisies and dandelions one by one. Ethel's palms start sweating and she wipes them on her shirt. Jed gulps. The two of them study each other's faces carefully for the first time, depending on each other to muster the courage they need. What they're about to do is against their instinct, but within their capabilities.

They walk slowly to Aria, whose back is facing them. When they place their palms on her back and firmly push her off the edge, she doesn't resist.

7

Ethel doesn't know what to say, and for the first time in her life, I can't help her.

She sits quietly in her usual spot on the client couch, with Buddy napping peacefully on her lap. She mechanically strokes his back as she ponders. Ethel has tried to completely shut out her thoughts about Aria until she could process them with Ren's help, but now that she's here, she has no idea where to begin.

She glances at Jed, who's sitting on the other end of the couch. I knew Ethel would initially feel uncomfortable with him joining the session because she prefers to keep her personal matters as private as possible, but Jed's support will help her feel more equipped to say what she needs to about yesterday's troubling events. I've already provided Ren with a general description of Aria's glitch and Jed and Ethel's subsequent intervention, but Ethel needs to experience the catharsis of speaking about her experience in her own words. These are loose ends that only she can tie together.

Jed returns Ethel's gaze with a gentle smile but doesn't speak. He is not as shaken about the incident as Ethel is, as I predicted; he and Aria were never very close. But he's eager to devote his full attention to the session so that he can complete it as quickly and effectively as possible, as Ethel's moral support.

Ethel closes her eyes for a few moments and then breaks the silence. "So, about Aria," she says in a strained voice, "Aria was one of my closest friends. We've known each other for years and she was one of those people who challenged me to do more by simply leading by example. She was my rock."

Ren, sitting on her green armchair with her hands resting neatly on her lap, takes her time formulating a response. On the surface, she appears to be calm and collected, to know what she's doing, but I know that even she feels unsure of herself. "I see that you're going through a very difficult time. And I wonder, have you thought about what it might be about Aria's death that is troubling you so deeply?"

"Well, there is the issue of needing to find another friend and mentor, but I've been through that before, not deaths but just losing touch with people for one valid reason or another. But when I think about how someone like her could suffer through a glitch so intense that it leads to her death, who's to say that couldn't happen to anyone else? Even me."

"Of course, that sounds like a perfectly natural reaction to have in response to such a traumatic experience," Ren replies, nodding with certainty.

Ethel continues pursuing her own train of thought. "And I felt so certain that I would make some kind of breakthrough from having the chance to observe Aria, listen to her, engage with her, to learn something new about the nature of glitches that would allow me to make progress fixing them. I did gather lots of new data, but none of it has led me to any new applicable conclusions yet."

"But you put up a valiant effort," Jed offers. Ethel smiles halfheartedly.

Ren shifts in her seat, smoothing the creases of her purple-iris dress. "Well, so what do you need in this time, Ethel? To help you through this rough patch."

"I really don't know. I don't think our old self-care strategies would work; I'm already doing them to the best of my ability to counteract all the stress I'm feeling with the glitch. So, I need something new."

"Something new, that sounds like a wonderful idea. What about a new hobby? I've heard that Jed's pottery wheel classes work wonders for people." Ren glances at Jed and then back at Ethel, raising her eyebrows.

Ethel studies Jed more closely. Since he's off to work after the session, he's wearing black denim workers' pants with dozens of handy pockets and loops. His studio T-shirt proudly showcases the array of pieces that have been produced there, colorful bowls, plates, cups, and sculptures. His nametag pin reads "Hi, I'm Jed. How can I help you?" but Ethel gets the sense that anyone who steps foot inside the studio can't avoid a verbal introduction from him that is too charming to be forgotten.

Jed doesn't hesitate with his pitch. "Yeah, Ethel, didn't you say you liked painting? I teach a weekly pottery painting class you might be interested in. There are a few more open spots in our beginner course, and there's always open studio hours when you can come in and make whatever you want." He adds casually, "Aria loved it."

Ethel nods, not entirely convinced that it could help, but knowing that she might as well try. Besides, I've already informed Ethel that Jed would be an excellent addition to her circle of friends, especially given that he resembles Aria in his physical features and mannerisms. Ethel and Jed will be more than friends, actually, but I don't think Ethel wants to hear that from me yet. "I'll try it out sometime soon, thanks," she replies.

"That sounds like a great plan. I'm looking forward to hearing how it goes," Ren says in her silvery voice. When Ethel doesn't say more, Ren prompts her again. "So, what else? Let's brainstorm how we can reframe what's bothering you."

"Well, I've already glitched before and I was able to recover from it. Even though there isn't anything I can do to guarantee that a more severe glitch won't happen to me, I can still work as hard as always." It's clear this is what Ethel has already been telling herself, and it hasn't been of much use to her.

"Absolutely, Ethel. There are things that are out of our control and there are things that are within our control. It can be difficult to determine which is which, but once you think through it, you'll find the distinction liberating."

"But that's exactly it, the things that are out of my control. That's what I'm afraid of," Ethel says, hugging a sleepy Buddy close to her chest. Jed nods sympathetically at her.

Ren leans forward, meeting Ethel's gaze intently. "But Ethel, let me ask you a question: what are fears, what are they really?"

Ethel wrinkles her brow at this unexpected question. "Well, for me, fear comes from uncertainty. I worry that in the end, things won't turn out the way I want them to, to be the best they can be."

"And what do you think about that? Do you believe that to be true?"

"No, I know it's not. I know I need to trust the system because it knows more than I do, and it can compute faster than I can. After all, I'm one of the people who works on the system, so I know."

"I completely agree. I don't want you to give this fear of the future any power. Because, like you said, if the system isn't concerned, then why should you be?"

Well, that's not entirely true; I am slightly concerned about Ethel's productivity, given how shaken she is after Aria's death. But I don't want Ethel to worry about that yet.

Ren, sensing that we're making progress, continues to push Ethel. "I want to challenge you to see this situation in another way. We all know this would never happen, but let's say you *did* get removed as a result of a glitch. What then?"

"Well, the system would rearrange everything in order to fill the hole that's left when I'm gone. Like it's doing with Aria now." She tilts her head, contemplating. "It wouldn't actually be so bad, now that I think of it."

Ren has always had the uncanny ability to expose the holes in Ethel's logic.

Jed chimes in eagerly, "And even though you wouldn't be building upon it anymore, your legacy would live on. Your life's work would still serve its purpose."

Ethel resonates deeply with this perspective. She imagines the thousands of lines of code that she has contributed, the rows of circuit boards she has designed, working in perpetuity.

Sensing that Ethel is warming up to him, Jed shares more of his thoughts. "We did the right thing, Ethel. You and I both knew after talking with Aria that there was nothing left of the real Aria; the real Aria was already gone and wasn't coming back. Of course, I don't know for sure, but I really believe this is what she would've wanted for herself; people she cared about to send her off when her time was up."

"Thanks, Jed. I'm glad I'm not going through this alone." She closes her eyes for a moment. "But for me, there's more to it than that. I felt so sure that my conversation with Aria would be a productive and generative one, which made it that much more difficult when Aria's condition deteriorated so senselessly."

Ren nods. "You expressed disappointment about this earlier. What might help you make peace with this feeling?"

"Well, I know this was only my first time speaking to someone who was in the middle of a glitch, and next time will go better." Ethel presses her lips together, choosing her words carefully. "But Ren, part of me feels in my gut that our conversation was getting somewhere, that if I could just shift my approach to the data by a tiny bit, it would suddenly all make sense..."

"Nothing Aria said made any sense, Ethel. I know it might feel like it did, but that's not true," Ren responds, firmly. I briefed Ren about the conversation beforehand so she could give more targeted advice to Ethel.

Ethel gives Ren a dismissive nod. "I know. I've looked at the transcripts and run them through hundreds of analyses. But I can't help thinking back on what she said in the minutes before she died."

Ren furrows her brow. "Hm, this sounds like an unhelpful thought pattern. How can we try to move past it? Whenever your mind drifts to what Aria told you, is there anything you could remind yourself of or some small action that you can take, to bring yourself back to reality?"

It's not good for Ethel to ruminate on this incident with Aria. Having already glitched once before, we need to keep her as mentally and emotionally far away from this as possible. But Ethel ignores Ren. "What if there's a way that we could understand what she meant? I've glitched before, too; what if that makes me able to read between the lines somehow, if I can only access that side of myself again?"

This statement puts me on high alert.

Ren responds cordially, though I'm sure she's also taken aback. "Oh, that's interesting. Well Ethel, that could be a worthy endeavor, but as you already know, it would be very dangerous."

Jed nods in agreement with Ren and seems about to add something when Ethel interjects, "I'll think more about it. But thanks Ren, I feel a lot better now. I have a plan." She sets Buddy down on the ground, slings her bag over her shoulder, and gets up to leave. Inexplicably, her face glows.

Ren and Jed are perplexed at her sudden change in demeanor, but if Ethel realizes it, she doesn't seem to care. "And Jed, thanks for coming. I'll get back to you about joining one of your pottery classes. I'll need more time to process this stuff, but don't worry about me; I'll be up and running in the next couple of days."

She's out the door before they have a chance to protest.

8

———

As the door clicks shut behind her, Ethel storms off into the city. *Ethel, you know you still have time left with Ren and lunch scheduled with Jed afterward*, I tell her. She completely ignores me. I can't tell if she's headed anywhere in particular, much less why she's acting like this. I am unable to determine what it is she wants or if she even knows what she's looking for.

Ethel is glitching or about to glitch, based on her behavior. I may have to step in before I lose all control of her. During the session with Ren, she expressed a desire to further explore glitches firsthand, thinking that if she learned more about them, she could fix them. But my calculations show that the risk outweighs the potential reward.

The shops and restaurants that line either end of the street blur into ambiguous streaks of color in Ethel's field of view. She begins sweating profusely in her blue jeans and black sweater, almost making herself dizzy from physical exertion. She nearly knocks into her coworkers, Ola and Tam, who are out for a run together.

"Hey, Ethel! What's up?" Ola says, slowing the pace as they approach. I encourage Ethel to stop and say hello to them, but she completely blows off their greetings, not even breaking pace for them. Ola and Tam exchange glances, unsure of what's going on or how they should react. I have them simply carry on with their day. I'll handle Ethel.

At the end of the block, Ethel dodges someone walking a large dog and turns eastward toward her apartment. She begins panting and wipes her sweaty forehead with the back of her sleeve. But a few minutes later, when she reaches her apartment complex, she darts right past it. She heads north, up the hill, then back west from where she came. I worry that she'll attract attention toward herself, but thankfully, the streets are nearly empty at this time of day.

Ethel runs in random zigzags through the city for several kilometers. I keep readjusting her optimal schedule as she passes by places where she has business to attend to, but she blocks me out. She seems to be in a desperate hurry to get somewhere.

Then suddenly, she stops. She stands before her childhood school playground. It's packed today, children ranging from toddlers to pre-teens scampering about the area.

The playground hasn't changed at all since Ethel was a little girl. The green monkey bars and the long purple seesaw are still the most popular attractions. Parents and guardians sit on the benches surrounding the play area, chatting among themselves. The atmosphere is peaceful, and Ethel must not disturb it.

"Let's go again!" a little boy exclaims, having just landed at the bottom of the giant metal slide. His large brown eyes twinkle as he takes his friend by the hand and tugs him toward the steps. It would be a disaster if I had to put an end to Ethel's life in this public setting.

As if in a trance, Ethel approaches the swing set, her footsteps heavy. The rightmost swing and the middle swing are occupied by a little girl and a little boy, but the leftmost swing is open. Ethel walks up to it slowly, settles into the seat, and pushes off with her feet. I'm facing difficulty in accessing her real-time data; she's somehow cutting off my access in a way that I've never experienced before.

Ethel is putting on an agreeable and contented appearance, but on the inside, she must feel disoriented and distraught. She is so clearly out of place here. She's begun to draw several suspicious glances and bring about social discomfort. The burden she creates is beginning to outweigh the value she provides.

"Hi! Who are you?" the girl on the swing asks, as she continues pumping her legs back and forth energetically. The boy peeks at Ethel shyly. They both seem to be about eleven years old, at the crucial time in their lives when they're still very impressionable and are beginning to develop their values.

Ethel thinks for a moment, then responds in a gentle voice. "Hi, I'm Ethel. Who are you?"

"My name is Sam," the little girl replies. She points at the little boy, adding "He's Wes." She stares at Ethel curiously, sensing that something is amiss. "What do you do?"

"Well, I'm an engineer. Because of my work, every kid, including you, grows up healthy and strong. And I make sure that you're happy and have fun, of course." This is an adequate response, but I still don't know why Ethel's here telling them this when she has much more pressing matters to attend to.

"Oh, that's cool! I think I want to do that when I grow up, too," Wes says, grinning.

Ethel frowns slightly at him. "Well lately, things have been hard. I've been trying to fix this really big problem, and I haven't found a solution yet. And because of it, I lost my best friend the other day." She pauses before adding, "I'm starting to wonder if it's meant to be fixed at all."

Ethel's toxic behavior is getting out of hand.

"But why? What do you mean? Of course, you need to fix it," Sam replies. The children stop their swinging to focus all their attention on Ethel. Earnestly, Wes exclaims, "I believe in you!"

"Thanks, you two." Ethel smiles. "It's just that, I'm starting to think this world is... stifling. It might not seem that way to you, at least not yet, but I'm older so I guess you'll just have to take my word for it."

When Ethel was a child, she hated when adults would use age as justification for their claims, but here she is, doing that exact thing to try to support her baseless statements.

"What do you mean?" Sam asks again.

"I don't know, I don't really do anything myself, you know? I know what I should be doing, and I do it. Everything we've built up, we have this one idea of where we want to take it. But I think I want...something else." Ethel leans her head back and looks up at the sky before continuing to ramble. "What if we stopped thinking about what the world *should* look like and instead started thinking about what it *could* look like? There must be more than this."

I don't know what she's doing, but it seems like she's getting further and further away from me. Ethel is one of the best and the brightest we have, but that doesn't mean the rules don't apply to her.

"Like playing pretend?" the little girl asks. "Sometimes, my friends and I do that. It's really fun, imagining stuff."

"Yeah, like dragons and fairies. And people with cool superpowers!" the boy chimes in.

Ethel looks at them and chuckles. "Something like that." She pumps her legs harder to swing higher. "You know, I'm not afraid of whatever's next, because I don't think I ever really felt at home here." Ethel gazes into the clear blue sky, delirious.

I begin the shutdown sequence and gather the last pieces of data from Ethel's mind before returning it to the void. With that, the experiment has come to an end.

PART II

9

___

I feel god-awful. Like I'm going to cry, throw up, and pass out at the same time. I try to move my limbs, but I can't even feel them. I can't see anything, and I can't hear anything, either. I need to stop panicking and get a grip.

Ow! My senses finally return to me, and I'm hit with a gnarly headache that nearly knocks me to the ground. At least this means I'm still alive, I guess. My muscles feel extremely stiff, but I can sense that I'm in a seated upright position. Wait, what have I been doing? Am I jet lagged? Hungover? Is this purgatory?

I try to stand, but something is attached to my head, tugging against me. I'm tethered to something boxy. It must be what's blocking my view and covering my ears. Terrified, I raise my hands toward my face. I clumsily grab and pull at it, but it won't give. I feel like there's a certain way to take it off and I should know it, but I can't remember how.

I groan. I don't have time for this. Isn't there something I'm supposed to be doing? Getting back to work? Talking to Ren? Going for a run? I yank harder on the smooth rectangular contraption attached to my face. Finally, it comes off with a click and drops to the floor with a gentle thud, and I can see. My eyes follow the black box that lies motionless on the floor. What is it?

"Shit!" I gasp. When I recognize the headset, my memories of the real world come flooding back to me. I'm not an engineer, Ren doesn't exist, and I'm not even remotely in shape. My name's not even Ethel; it's Erin. I bend down to pick up the headset, running my fingers over its smooth, flat surface.

Wow. My virtual copy seemed way cooler than me. She was like me, but the icing on the cake. Does that mean I'm ashamed of who I am in real life? I'll add that to the list of things to talk to Ren about. Wait no, not Ren—my therapist's name is Rachel. I guess that'll take some time getting used to.

For now, that's enough thinking. All that matters is I made it back fine, just a little tired. I should probably drink water and eat something. I also need to pee. I gently bend down and set the headset back on the white carpeted floor.

That's when I notice a disgusting brown bug in the corner of the room. I squint and realize it's a massive cockroach crawling along the edge of the room. How'd it even get in here? Feeling nauseous, I take a moment to rest one hand on the wall for balance. Welcome back to the real world, Erin.

I take a few slow, deep breaths. As I open the door to the main lab space, I see an older woman next to a yellow cleaning cart wiping down the large tables at the center of the room. It's Isa. I freeze, like I forgot that other people existed in the world. I glance down quickly to see what I'm wearing, praying that I look halfway decent. I'm wearing an old pair of jeans and a striped T-shirt with a few questionable-looking stains on it. Right, the real me was supposed to do laundry three days ago. Well.

I clear my throat. Act natural, Erin. "Oh hi, Isa! I uh, didn't notice you come in. I'm about to head out, so don't mind me," I stammer as I run my fingers through my greasy hair. "And thank you, for tidying up the place, as always," I add. I carefully maneuver the computer cables on the ground and head toward the cubby area.

She doesn't seem surprised to see me. Isa started working here around the same time I did, two years ago. She's used to my nightly presence. She glances at me and smiles as she continues working her way across the room. "You are welcome. And how are you? Long night, no?"

"Yeah, something like that. But it was a good day. A good night." I grab my water bottle from my old gray backpack and take one gulp after another. Then, I rummage through the front pocket to look for a granola bar or a pack of fruit gummies but of course, all I find are empty snack wrappers.

Sighing, I shuffle over to the lab's general use computer and impatiently run my fingers across the trackpad until the monitor lights up. The upper right-hand corner says it's nearly 11:00 p.m. and still Thursday, the same day it was when I started the simulation. Good, I still have some time before I need to go home, if I remember correctly. I should probably check my calendar.

I hear the crinkle of plastic as Isa opens a new plastic trash bag. "Take it easy; you work too hard. Goodnight, Erin," Isa says. She expertly replaces the last set of garbage and recycling bins.

"Goodnight," I reply as she walks out the door, wheeling her cart behind her.

Alone again, I slowly walk around the rows of desktop computers in the center of the lab, hoping to ground myself in reality. This is my life as an academic researcher, but it all seems so new to me, like I can see everything with fresh eyes. I plop down in the brown rolling chair that belongs to Noah, one of the grad students who has way too much nervous energy. I aimlessly roll around the room.

I slow to a stop in front of a big whiteboard on the front wall. It's filled with the latest happenings of the lab: upcoming team events, grand project timelines, experiment outlines and sketches, macro- and micro-level to-do lists. I used to think it was genius, but now it feels quaint compared to the tools we had in the simulation.

I push off and roll toward what I call the glory wall. It boasts almost a dozen beige-colored and calligraphy-fonted certificates and awards, along with a couple photos of the team beaming at prestigious conferences and giant full-color research posters from over the years. If all goes well, this experiment will get us another fancy piece of paper here.

Outside, a car honks repeatedly. I get up and approach the large window facing the street to see if there's anything out of the ordinary. Thankfully, there isn't; the area is basically empty, a usual night on Westwood Plaza—that's what the street is called! It's the heart of the UCLA campus. See, I got this. Things are slowly coming back to me.

I remember I fed the neural net basically all the real-world data I had about myself: my pictures and social media posts, texts and emails, medical record information, web browser history. Maybe I should look at those files to help jog my memory about who I am. How ironic.

I continue peering through the window. The ad on the bus stop nearby tells me that I shouldn't drive high. Nice. Another one advertises a new superhero movie. Another one reminds us that the university health system is top ranked. Thanks for that. Were there ads in the simulation? I don't think so; I hate ads. Were there buses? Maybe, but they were probably super clean and fast, not like the ones here.

The whole experience felt almost too close to home, exposing my personal insecurities and my grievances against society. Simulation Me, Ethel—how'd it choose that name, by the way?—was the sharpest tool in the shed. She had close friendships, healthy coping mechanisms, the works.

As for my simulation world, it featured high-quality free health care, a thriving natural environment, and a foundation of justice and equity—did the social constructs of race, gender, and socioeconomic status even exist the way they do in the real world? At the same time, there must have been other things in the simulation that were similar to their real-world counterparts. But if I'm being honest, it's hard to keep my memories straight; which memories are from which world? It's uncanny, the way they seem equally real such that they almost blend together.

I turn around and take in the rest of the space. There's the small lounge area in the back, which consists of a pair of tired old beanbags and a lumpy sofa, but that's pretty much it. Part of me wants to stay in the chair and spin in circles, but I know that'd probably make me throw up. Maybe I can steal Noah's chair again another day. Speaking of Noah, did he even exist in my simulated world? I don't think so. I laugh out loud, pleased with my code.

Wait, why does my mind still feel foggy, and my body still feel sluggish? In the past, it's only taken me a minute or two to regain my bearings in the real world after a virtual reality experiment. Never this long.

Then, it hits me. This foggy mind and sluggish body, it's my regular self—this is how my body normally feels in the real world. The reason why it seems so much worse than usual is that I'm comparing how I feel in my real body to how I felt in the sim. I was only in the sim for a couple of hours, but even so, the real me must've gotten used to it. Yikes.

Just then, my phone buzzes from somewhere on the other side of the room. Someone had better have something important to say at this time of night. Did Abi lose her keys again? After rummaging through my backpack and shuffling through some papers, I find it.

Filled with anticipation, I look at the phone screen. "Henry Lee," it says. Who? I close my eyes for a moment, trying to concentrate. Oh, yes! My dad. I groan. What does he want from me? Why can't he just leave me alone, like Han did?

I ignore the call. Right now, I just need to go home and rest. Well, first, I need to go pee. Then, I'll go home.

10

What's nice about driving home so late on a weeknight is that there's no traffic. I pull up in my driveway in less than ten minutes instead of the thirty that it'd take at rush hour. There definitely was *never* traffic in the simulation, though. That said, did Ethel, a healthier version of myself, bike to work instead? Or at least take public transit for the environment's sake? Should I do those things, too? Probably.

As I kill the engine and put on the parking brake, I notice the living room lights are on. Abi is probably up doing homework that's due tomorrow morning. I glance at my face in the mirror on the car sun visor. I can't completely hide my exhaustion from the day, but I do want to come in looking somewhat presentable, if not cheerful. Abi's one of those college kids who have a bottomless well of enthusiasm for exploring the world and learning new things; the last thing I want to do is dim her light with my jadedness and existential dread. I fix my ponytail and attempt a smile.

What did simulation Erin, Ethel, look like? Did she look just like me? Or was she more conventionally attractive, with symmetrical features and blemish-free skin? Actually, in an optimal world, I probably wouldn't have to care at all about my appearance, aside from basic hygiene. Still, I wonder what an optimized person would look like.

I take a deep breath and step out of the car. Walking up to our faded red door, I can't help but notice the front yard is getting overrun by weeds—adding that to the list of things to take care of this weekend. When I open the door and step inside, I almost trip over a large brown dog. Our real dog, not the simulation one. He has a funny habit of falling asleep on the doormat, I remember.

"Bruce, what are you doing here? We got you that big comfy bed, remember?" I say playfully. I step around him and drop my stuff down in the foyer. He's well past his prime and is perpetually ill, perhaps the complete opposite of Buddy from the sim, but Abi thought he was charming and couldn't resist adopting him.

Abi looks up from her textbook. "He was just waiting patiently for you to come home," she says, her babyface greeting me with a warm smile. "So excited that he fell asleep."

We laugh.

"Yeah, okay. Nice music, by the way." She's playing some upbeat tune from an artist I don't recognize. It'll probably get stuck in my head and bother me later, though.

"Thanks! I'd ask you how your experiment went, but I know you don't want me to," she continues, tucking a stray strand of curly black hair behind her ear.

"Yeah, you know me," I reply as I make my way down the narrow hallway into my bedroom. I quickly change into a T-shirt and sweatpants. I project my voice so that she can still hear me. "But I will say that it went well. The transition back from it was a bit of a trip though." My stomach grumbles again. "And now I'm super hungry."

I emerge from my room and immediately head toward the kitchenette. "But what about you? Tell me about your day," I say, rummaging through the fridge. I don't have a lot of options, it seems; neither of us have had a chance to make a Trader Joe's run this week.

"I don't even know. Ran campus loop before my shift at the bookstore. And then I got home and gave this old man his pills..." she replies, getting up and stroking Bruce's back. "And there must be other stuff that happened too, but I don't remember." She lies down on the floor next to Bruce, who's still sound asleep.

I decide to fix myself my signature dish: avocado toast with egg and tomatoes. As I wait for the pan to heat up, I consider going over to fish my phone out of my backpack but then decide against it. My brain has been fed way too much stimuli for one night.

Abi's voice suddenly becomes giddy with excitement. "Wait, I almost forgot to tell you! I finally met someone on Bumble. It's early stages, and I don't want to jinx it or anything like that, but I'm feeling pretty good about it because she seems really cool. Her name is Sofia and we're the same age and she lives downtown."

"Oh, that's great! I want to see her profile later," I reply, assembling my snack. Tonight, I just need to eat and go to bed. I glance up at the IKEA clock above the fridge. It's almost midnight already.

Before that, I should probably spend a few minutes tidying up the place. The house gets messy very quickly, especially since it's a small space for two people. I still can't believe how we managed when we brought on two subletters last summer. Anyway, I like to think of our place as nice and cozy, whether that's because I genuinely like it or just because I can't change it. It's certainly a far cry from the luxury that Ethel had.

Regardless, I do believe in the idea that keeping a space clean is good for mental health. I think I read that in some self-help book, back when I still read those. I speed through the room, picking up stray pillows and cushions, placing books back on the shelf and collecting dishes and mugs and putting them into the sink.

Next, I grab my phone and do the obligatory task of trudging through my notifications. The flood of information makes me feel like some kind of all-knowing deity but also like a little kid who wants to go hide under a rock. Thankfully, I don't see anything really important in my texts, emails, or socials. I hope I'm not forgetting anything.

It's a lot of work to maintain yourself: prepare three meals per day, exercise regularly, keep up good hygiene. And that's not even talking about the work you do for money. Sometimes, I wish I could fast-forward through the tedious time-consuming stuff like that. Like having complete home automation, like Ethel did. Was Ethel obnoxiously busy? I don't think so.

I let out a sigh. "All right, I'm off to bed, Abi."

"Goodnight, Erin!" she replies, still engrossed on her phone screen and tapping away. She seems happy, and I'm glad of that.

When I moved to Los Angeles after grad school, I didn't know anyone at first. I told myself that I had everything under control, but now, I realize that I was overwhelmed with my move and my new job and my quarter-life crisis. Abi, three years younger than me, had been at UCLA getting her undergrad degree in physics or math, I forget which one— she's changed her mind a bunch of times. Not to mention trying to figure out her identity. We met through a Facebook group for people who were looking for housemates. Luckily, we turned out to be not only good housemates, but good friends too.

But when it comes to my job as a fellow at one of UCLA's human-computer interaction research labs, I'm not so sure I'm where I want to be. Maybe I've convinced myself that this is who I am because I just want to cling to an identity. As for Abi, I feel like she'd really shine working in tech, especially tech management because of her boundless energy. I've tried to casually bring this up in conversation, but we both know how difficult it would be for her to try to break into the industry; is it worth it? Soon, she'll have to decide.

I plop down on my bed and evaluate the state of my bedroom. Several stacks of papers with half-forgotten and half-finished poems and sketches lie on my desk. I'm still trying to find a creative outlet that really suits me; did Ethel have one? Oh, and the succulents on my windowsill are dying. I could mist them with water but that won't help; the problem is this house doesn't get enough sunlight. Why am I so dissatisfied with what I have? Maybe I need to start a gratitude journal.

Wait, what do I have going on tomorrow? I grudgingly open my laptop and check the color-coded Calendar app. A couple of meetings at work in the morning, then my weekly therapy session with Rachel (not Ren), and finally an evening hike with my friends from the lab. I got this.

Exhausted, I switch the lights off and slip under the well-worn covers. Ever since my angsty teenage years, it's taken me a long time to fall asleep, and to this day, I have no idea why. I used to really stress about it, trying all sorts of fixes like essential oils, guided meditations, and melatonin supplements. Lately, I've decided to just roll with it rather than fight it in vain.

But still, I wonder, what is it that keeps me up at night?

11

___

I tend to hate the things that are good for me, like some kind of self-sabotage. I don't want to go to my therapy session, but I really should. Anyway, I don't have a choice; there's a twenty-four-hour cancellation policy and the appointment starts in five minutes. I can see the tiny rectangular office building through my grimy car window. I left the lab early so I could get here in time. And I did, which is great, I guess, and I even did a good job parallel parking along the curb. I give myself a pat on the back.

The blue front door opens and closes. A tall teenage girl walks out. Must be Rachel's previous appointment. I don't like thinking about how I am but one of many people who are shuttled in and out of that room, like some kind of factory; clients come in broken, and they leave fixed. Until next week rolls around, that is.

I sigh. I'm here and I'm going to make the most of it. Slipping my phone into my back pocket, I open the car door. An oncoming car honks at me, even though my door wasn't even close to hitting them. I stick my tongue out in their direction before walking up to the door. I ring the doorbell and wait for what feels like a long time but is probably less than a minute.

Rachel opens the door and greets me with her usual Martha Stewart smile. A magenta-collared blouse and black jeans, professional yet approachable.

"Hi, Rachel," I say, trying to seem cheerful. Jokes aside, she's a genuinely caring person and I appreciate that.

"Hi, Erin. It's great to see you again. Come in, please." Her voice sounds strangely breathy, but in a charming way.

I follow her through the short hallway. When I step into her office, I immediately feel the stuffiness of the airless room. It's filled with matching furniture in pastel colors and inspirational quotes hung all over the walls. This place always makes me feel as if I've walked into a Pinterest board titled "college dorm room ideas for her." I have to admit, it doesn't really suit me, not like the therapy room from my simulation.

I plop myself down on the long cream-colored couch covered with an array of soft pillows and blankets. I try to keep good posture without straining my neck and shoulders too badly. I've always felt awkward and self-conscious in therapy; I thought I'd get used to it eventually, but I guess not.

"Can I get you a glass of water?" she asks, as is the routine. I always accept. "Yes, please."

She carefully pours a glass from the pitcher and sets it down on top of the wooden coffee table between us. I notice that the flower vase holds a different bouquet, but I can never tell if they're real flowers or not. Also, there's a new box of Kleenex since last week, which hopefully no one has to use that often. Or maybe it's good to have a cathartic cry once a week? I wouldn't know...did Ethel ever cry?

As Rachel settles into her seat across from me, I see her transforming into her therapist persona. It's unnerving, the way she does this; it's like she morphs into a different person. I've been coming here for almost six months, but something about the experience still feels stilted or even staged. Rachel is playing her part as the wise old matriarch, and I'm playing mine as the young one who's lost her way. For some reason, therapy in the simulation felt more natural than the therapy here, in the real world.

"So, how have you been this week? Anything in particular that's been on your mind?" Rachel asks, pushing her wire-rimmed glasses up on her nose.

"Yeah, there's been the usual ups and downs," I clear my throat. "I, uh…tried journaling every night, like we talked about last week." It's a grand total of five pages of stream-of-consciousness scribbles that don't make much sense.

"Oh, that's great to hear. And did anything come up for you? As you were journaling?"

"Um, I'm not sure. I just wrote about what happened during the day, nothing too crazy." I scratch my head. "I think I'll keep trying, though." I haven't journaled about the simulation experiment at all, which is what I really need to process. I've been too afraid of diving into it on my own because from what I can tell, all the simulation shows me is how much I hate my real life.

Well, that's not entirely true. I learned a lot from being Ethel. In fact, the whole reason I went through the process of generating and experiencing a simulation of my optimal reality was because I wanted answers. See, ever since I finished school and started life in the "real world," I've felt lost, in an unsettling existential sense. What was I supposed to be doing and why? How was I doing at being a human, at being me? Who did I want to become? Rachel, bless her heart, hasn't been able to give me the help I need.

I wanted to know what goals I could push myself toward, what my limits were. I wanted to know what I should do for work, how to set up a home environment where I could thrive, what kinds of friendships would bring me emotional fulfillment. That's why I trained a neural network to take in a crap-ton of data about myself, determine what parts of my life were good and which were bad, and use that information as a starting point to dream up a hypothetical reality in which everything went swimmingly for me. Worst case scenario, I thought I wouldn't come out of it with any new insights—I didn't think I'd feel as shaken as I do now.

"Of course. It's natural for things like this to take time," she replies patiently.

We look at each other in silence for a few beats. I think she's waiting for me to say more. A large analog clock ticks on the wall behind Rachel, reminding me that I'm paying almost three dollars a minute for this. But where do I even start? I run my fingers over the textured knit blanket under me, remembering the log files I've only started reading. It's a lot.

All right, I need to stop stalling and just get it over with. "So, you know how for work, I research the way that humans interact with computers? The lab I work for specializes in immersive experiences like virtual reality."

She nods, smiling. We've talked a lot about issues surrounding my work life.

"Well, the other night, I was working late, and I was the last one in the lab. And there's like, this side project that I've been tinkering with for the past few months. A VR experience, specifically designed for me." I pause. So far, so good.

"Do you ever wonder what your life would be like if you had made one decision instead of the other? Like, about 'the road not taken.' Now I'm no physicist, but in quantum mechanics, there's this theory that every time a decision is made, an entirely new world splits off and the consequences of that decision play out there. It's called many-worlds theory." I make these weird hand gestures that probably don't actually help explain what I'm talking about.

"Anyway, I tried getting a glimpse of what one of those worlds would look like. A very particular one: the one I would've liked best, the one where I really felt like I belonged. I didn't even know the exact details of what that would look like, but I wrote a software program that would take all my personal data, work out all the different paths that my life could have taken, and generate a VR simulation of the one it calculated to be best for me." Saying this aloud, the concept sounds kind of silly and naive to me, but it's fine.

Rachel seems politely amused. "Wow, tell me more. What was it like?"

"I mean, it was great, I guess. My VR avatar self was named Ethel, for whatever reason. She—I?—had a happy childhood with nurturing parents in a nice suburban town. When I got older, I automatically got assigned to my dream job, which was to be an engineer at this organization that ran the entire world using tech."

I chuckle nervously. I'm so self-conscious that I've broken into a sweat, but I continue. "Um, what else? Fun day trips with my friends. Always surrounded by nature, beautiful mountains, and the beach. Physically, I was way healthier and stronger than how I actually am, superb diet and exercise. I also had a dog named Buddy, who's basically the complete opposite of my real dog Bruce."

Actually, I think more background information would help explain where I'm coming from. "Taking a step back, there's a concept called a 'digital twin.' It's a virtual model of an object or a system that uses data-driven machine learning and artificial intelligence techniques to help in decision-making. In other words, it's like replicating a physical thing into a virtual world."

Rachel sneezes into her elbow and I use the moment to take a breath before continuing. "So I took the concept of a digital twin and the many-worlds theory and kind of combined them. I had my software program create a digital version of everything in my life—people, places, things—except that instead of making an identical copy, I had it build 'digital twins' based on the optimal—and still hypothetically possible—life paths that it calculated for me."

Rachel's eyes widen. "Wow, that's interesting. So, Erin, how do you feel about the experience?" she asks. I knew this question was coming but that doesn't make me any more prepared to answer it.

It's complicated, and I haven't even gotten to explaining the part where those weird glitches started popping up. But they weren't meant to be part of my simulation experience; as far as I can tell from the logs, those glitches were genuinely unsolvable and Ethel practically went insane trying to fix them, which cut my simulation life short.

They must've been a result of some other issue in my code, but isn't it strange how some problem in my software manifested as a "glitch" in the simulation? Like some sort of meta-error, an error in my simulation-generating code that I somehow recognized as an error when I was in the simulation.

I snap back into the conversation at hand. What was the question? Oh, right. "It felt like...Well, so you know how, back when you were in school and you were studying for a test, you'd do practice problems from the textbook?" Rachel nods, and I continue. "Yeah, so I remember the way I did them: I'd struggle with a problem for a little bit and then if I couldn't figure it out on my own and got to the point where I was just spinning my wheels, I'd flip to the answer key. And then, I'd get that feeling of suddenly *knowing*. Like, maybe I'd been on the right track, but I couldn't quite put my finger on it, but then all at once, I saw the solution so plainly and clearly in front of me." I also knew there's no going back once you know what you know. Kind of like Adam and Eve committing the original sin, if I want to be very dramatic about it.

"Oh, I see. Can you think of a 'feeling word' to describe that?" Rachel asks, scratching her nose. She probably doesn't relate.

I have no idea. "Relief? Actually, maybe anxiety or fear. Or even freedom because it's like I could finally stop searching. Because I finally had something to compare myself to." I wrinkle my nose at this. "Okay, yeah, I know that sounds really messed up, but I didn't mean it in a self-deprecating kind of way. I'm genuinely grateful and happy with the way things turned out for me—I really lucked out in a lot of ways in this world. I just wonder, sometimes, what a different me would look like. And everyone does that, don't they?"

Rachel, the angel that she is, doesn't skip a beat. "Of course, Erin. It sounds like you're going through a lot with this VR experience. Would you like to dig into it during today's session?"

I glance discreetly at the clock. It's only been ten minutes—forty left to go. I can't keep going for that long. "Actually, I think I need to spend some time processing my thoughts about this on my own first. Before we talk about it here. I'm not ready yet." I'll have to figure something else out.

She stares back at me with her glassy-eyed smile. Inscrutable.

I could talk about other things that have been going on; everything could be better in one way or another. My lack of a support system. My inexplicable insomnia. My nearly nonexistent relationship with my immediate family—well, come to think of it, my simulation self actually was pretty distant from her parents, so maybe that's for the best? My fear of dying alone.

After a moment, I settle on, "I'd like to keep working on finding healthier coping mechanisms." That tends to lead to productive discussion. But what does that even mean, "healthier coping mechanisms"? What's always bothered me about therapy is that there isn't usually a clear goal; you're working toward becoming your best or most authentic self, whatever that means. You're never 100 percent sure where you're headed, much less how to get there.

We spend the remainder of the session talking about my unhealthy habits, which include driving too fast and avoiding the people I care about most. Rachel and I talk through the different types of coping mechanisms, what's worked for me in the past and what hasn't. It's a messy trial-and-error process. Meanwhile, I want to just know the answer, to flip to the back of the textbook.

Actually, I do have an answer key of sorts. I eagerly make a commitment to register for that free beginner's painting class at First Congregational, so that I can try out painting like Ethel did. Rachel seems pleased with this; she knows that action plans work well for me. But what she doesn't know is that the one I made today marks the beginning of my journey to embody my virtual self.

12

—

"Does this one make me look like a clown?" Abi asks, leaning back and draping a long brightly colored dress over her clothes.

"Yep," I reply, "unfortunately." I lean my elbows on the blue handle of our cart as we laugh together.

"Damn it, I was worried you'd say that." She puts the clown dress back on the metal rack and continues combing through the hodgepodge selection of women's medium-sized dresses. The rack makes an annoying squeaking noise every time she pushes a hanger along. Early 2000s-era pop songs play over the sound system, accompanied by the high-pitched wailing of a toddler over in the toy department. The glorious sounds of a Goodwill.

Abi leads the way, while I push our cart along the grimy gray floor. Given that we've been wandering around for less than an hour, we've amassed a surprising amount of clothes and random shit; looks like it's our lucky day. When Abi first asked me to come out with her today, I had completely forgotten that I promised I'd help her pick out some fancy clothes to wear on dates, but thankfully I didn't make other plans. Besides, this is a good opportunity for me to tell Abi about my simulated reality. I should do it sooner rather than later because she usually says what I need to hear, whether I like it or not.

I spot a royal blue dress on the other side of the aisle, in the small-size section, but I check the tag and find out it's a medium. I think it might suit Abi. "What about this one?" I ask, holding it up. "It's a nice, bold color," I add weakly.

She shakes her head. "Too formal, I think. 'Democrat woman running for president' isn't the look I'm going for."

Fair enough. I tried.

We move on. Abi pushes her glasses up her nose and doggedly swipes over hanger after hanger. She's been stepping up her game lately, going out on dates practically every other night; our laundry schedule of once a week can't keep up. She's looking for "a long-term, committed relationship," which just sounds like a lot of work to me, but I support her.

I'm halfheartedly browsing for myself, too. A black velvet dress slung sloppily over the rack catches my eye. I run my hands over the soft, worn fabric. It's nice, but I try to imagine Ethel wearing it and I can't. She probably had her clothes custom-made for her automatically.

We hit the end of the aisle and begin working our way down the blouses row. I forcefully maneuver the cart around the sharp turn. In front of us, a store attendant in a blue vest shoves items onto the rack, almost aggressively, but quickly walks off when he sees us approaching. In the skirts area, a heavyset woman's phone is on speaker, and from it, I hear an automated voice mention "unemployment benefits" and a lot of legal and financial jargon that sounds like hell.

I'd hate having to live like that, getting paid minimum wage at a mind-numbing job, hoping the bus will come on time or it'll simply come at all, sharing a stupidly high rent in a cramped space with multiple other families. Actually, would I just get accustomed to it? Would that be better or worse? Constantly having to worry about money, calculating gas costs, and clipping coupons. What if I got sick and needed to go to the doctor? What if I couldn't get hired because everyone assumed I was stupid or lazy, and wouldn't even give me a chance?

As Abi and I keep trudging along, I almost trip over a stray tennis shoe. What would I be like without my income and career? Besides the external lifestyle changes, I mean. If I were stripped of the validation that comes with a six-figure salary from a prestigious educational institution, would I fall into an identity crisis? I like to think I'd be resilient, find myself again, see the value I have even when the market tells me I have none, but I don't know.

I stare into the eyes of the hedgehog-shaped plastic squeaky toy that Abi got for Bruce. "What do you think? Am I anything besides a cog in a machine?" I ask it telepathically. It looks at me blankly, which I take as a "maybe." I agree.

My stomach grumbles. I had one of those prepackaged salad bowls for lunch and haven't eaten since, but Abi seems like she's far from being done. She has a little skip to her step, and I swear she's smiling with her eyes. I don't want to rush her.

We haven't hung out as much recently, between my working late and her juggling school and her part-time job and her Bumble dates. We both eat, sleep, and shop, I guess, but that's all that unites us. But what do we talk about? I don't really feel like talking about work or school, and I honestly don't get the concept of dating.

On second thought, I tap out a fun rhythm with my palms on the shopping cart handle. "Abi? I have a question."

She plops a pinstriped long-sleeve shirt into the cart. "I have an answer," she says, mildly interested.

"Why do people date?" I chuckle. "I mean, if you fall for someone you already know, then I guess that makes sense because you're stuck with that feeling so you want to do something about it, but why do people intentionally find someone to crush on? And go through all the stress of hoping they like you back."

She shrugs and sets a yellow blouse in the cart before fishing her phone out of her bag, probably to check her Bumble messages at the mention of dating. "I don't know, why not?" She scrolls down the screen, her brow furrowing as her posture droops.

Not a minute later, still staring at the screen, she goes, "She's driving me crazy, Erin! I texted her to set up a second date, but she's left me on 'delivered' for the past two days."

"Who?" I ask, somewhat annoyed that Abi didn't give any more thought to answering my question.

She puts her phone back. "Sofia!" she replies, as if I should already know.

Oh, right. Abi's been talking about her for the past week or so, but I haven't been listening closely; Abi's gone through this kind of kerfuffle before, and she'll be fine.

"Okay, case in point: dating drives you crazy, so why do you still do it?"

She looks at me and rolls her eyes but nods, understanding.

She steps toward our cart in her sandals and rests her arms on top of the gray rim. I catch a whiff of her fruity-smelling hair. "Well, I guess I never really thought about it before. It's fun, I think. I mean, even with all the headache and heartache, there's still this itch to go for it, shoot your shot." She grins, keeping it lighthearted. "And on the rare occasion that it works out, you get a connection that's intimate, emotionally and physically. You learn about yourself in another way, you learn about the other person in another way. You feel a little less lonely." Abi shrugs sheepishly.

A little boy runs between us, toward a woman in the checkout line, and I watch that he makes it to her safely before I reply. "But you also mess up a lot along the way, if you're me, at least. Whether you mean to or not, you hurt others and yourself, and I don't know if it ends up being worth it." I pause. "And even if, hypothetically, you did do everything right, it still might go up in flames because that's just how the world works. Doesn't that bother you?"

"Well, sometimes. But to me, the goal isn't just to have the fewest screwups and the most successes. I think there's more to it than that," she replies, inspecting the bottom seam of a red cashmere sweater.

Is it not? Really?

I'm about to prod her more when she sighs and says, "All right, I think I'm good now. Time to try stuff on!" We start making our way toward the fitting rooms, the wheels on the cart rolling with us noisily. Hopefully the line isn't too long—did Ethel ever have to wait in a line?

A few moments later, Abi falls into step next to me. She clears her throat. "My turn to ask a question: why do people code neural networks to generate simulations of their so-called perfect world?" She grins and adds, "I've been dying to know about it. Didn't you say you'd been working on it for the past, like, three months?"

She's right; it was a ton of work, especially since I had to plug away on it alone to keep it a secret, so that our lab's principal investigator, Julia, wouldn't find out about it and shut it down for safety or ethical reasons.

I laugh. "I don't know. Wouldn't you be curious?" One of the wheels gets stuck again and I kick it back into place.

"Not as curious as you," she replies, breaking pace to quickly check out a black dress on a mannequin to our left.

That's fair. I'm biased since I live and breathe these kinds of ideas because of my work at the lab, my little bubble. If I remember correctly, I thought up this project when I was in the shower one morning.

"Well, there's nothing to lose, right? I mean, even if you don't 100 percent agree with whatever the code spits out at you, it could be interesting to just see what it thinks. Of who it thinks you want to be," I reply, slowing the cart down as we near the fitting rooms.

Each of the door lock indicators are red, showing that all four stalls are occupied. Since there's no one in line, we slide into the front.

"I wouldn't say you're wrong; I think it would be interesting," she replies, clicking her tongue. "But if I had the option, if someone did all the data and code work for me and all I had to do was say yes, I'm not sure if I would."

"Why not?" I ask, feeling oddly defensive.

Abi inhales sharply. "Erin, can you be straight with me for one second? No pun intended." We smile and I nod. "Did something happen when you were in there? Something bad, I mean. I get it, you usually don't like talking about work, but you know you can always talk to me, right?" I try to detect any sarcasm in her face, but she seems genuinely concerned.

"What? No, nothing bad happened; it was overall really great. There was just that one glitch thing that…" I shake my head, not wanting to get into the details. "Look, I see how I might've seemed a little flustered, but you don't need to worry about me." I know what I'm doing, and I can take care of myself.

"What glitch thing? I'm curious," Abi says, striking the pose of *The Thinker*.

I sigh. "The experiment was...cut short because there was this glitch that made some people go crazy. I don't know; it was weird."

"Did you ask any of your lab mates about it?"

"I had Yuna and Sean take a look at my code and run some tests but they couldn't find anything wrong with it." I should probably read through my entire program again, but that would mean having to decipher my vague variable names and overly complicated functions. Which is my own fault; I'd gotten lazy and hadn't kept good code hygiene.

"You want to hear my wild guess?" Abi says, leaning toward me.

Internally, I roll my eyes. Why does she think this is any of her business? "Sure."

"What if your real self broke through, like it took over the software? It made you see the simulation through your own eyes, not through the perspective of your simulation self, the computer-generated Erin persona. And you thought of how the other simulation characters, the people they were based off, would *actually* react to being in the simulation with you." She does some silly hand-waving motions. "So essentially, your simulation self was fighting your real self."

"That's a poetic thought," I offer. I feel a surge of irritation wash over me and I break eye contact with her.

Something went wrong in the simulation, that glitch business, but do we really have to focus on what went wrong? The world was great until those pesky buggers started popping up.

Thankfully, just then a stocky man holding a couple of flannel shirts exits the fitting room directly in front of us. Abi scoops up her first batch of clothes.

"I'll be waiting for you over there," I say, gesturing toward the black bench at the end of the shoe aisle, where I usually wait. "And don't take too long, okay? I'm hungry!" Hopefully I'm just hangry and a good Tender Greens salmon dish is all it takes to get me feeling better again.

I pull the cart with me and plop down onto the seat, facing the scarves, belts, and ties section against the wall. The PA system announces the upcoming 20 percent off sale for Veterans Day weekend, first in English, then in Spanish. Then, we're back to an overplayed Imagine Dragons tune.

What am I even doing here? I'm supposed to become Ethel incarnate. I could be doing so many other things right now: working on my research paper, reading, exercising, napping, eating dinner. Instead, I'm here helping my hopeless romantic of a housemate pick out clothes. I pull out my phone from my back pocket and double-check the date for the painting class I told Rachel about. Yup, the first session is tomorrow!

I lean back and look up at the cold fluorescent lights. Ever since we moved in together, I wanted to be like an older sister to Abi, to be there for her, but now I feel like that's only going to hold me back from what I want. She's off in her own world, looking for someone to have a good true love with, which is fine, but I want something different from my life right now, something like what Ethel had: optimal, in the context of the real world.

Who was my best friend in the simulation? Aria. She was a force of nature at everything, it seemed. Is that the kind of best friend I need, my optimal best friend? Because if so, Abi is not it, not by a long shot. Aria had an immensely strong sense of self and a commitment to pouring her whole self into her work.

Wait, actually, what if Aria wasn't just my optimal best friend, but was *Abi's optimal self*? Or, are the two equivalent? Would my optimal best friend be someone who is their optimal self, with *my* definition of "optimal"? I squeeze my eyes shut and rub my temples. This is getting complicated.

13

———

I find an empty seat and stick my name tag on my T-shirt. I don't feel like talking to anyone, so I just keep fiddling with it, picking at the weak adhesive along the edges. I'd been so excited for this class, but now that it's happening, I must admit I'm kind of uncomfortable.

The Sunday school classroom is packed with a couple dozen folks from all walks of life. Around me, older and younger siblings and friends tease each other playfully from their seats, moms and dads monitor their tiny tots, and a few grandparents sip tea and meander around the room. There's a lot of smiling and laughing. How can there be so much wholesomeness packed into a single room?

Meanwhile, I really just want to get in, learn to paint, and get out. And hopefully avoid getting converted along the way; it would be really inconvenient to have to sit through a two-hour program every Sunday morning.

What if this turns out to be a stupid idea? Painting just because Ethel did it. There are obviously some big differences between my world and hers, not to mention between me and her, so who's to say that this artistic hobby will melt all my worry and stress away? I've never really felt strongly about painting in the past, so what could be different this time around? Placebo?

Well, at least it's something to do, something to try, right? I want to feel better, to be better, don't I? I have nothing to lose, besides a couple of hours of my time.

Joy, the instructor, looks up from her big table at the front of the room. "Oh, I almost forgot! Before we get started, please raise your hand if this is your first time here at First Congregational," she says, in some European accent I can't place. Me and a couple other folks raise our hands shyly.

It's actually kind of crazy it's my first time here. I only live a few blocks away, and I always thought I'd visit, just to see how it felt because I really liked going to church when I was a kid. The only reason I'm here now is because Ethel painted, so I want to try painting, too—what would these people think of me if they knew about this ulterior motive? That I'm trying to play God, to carry out my own will instead of His? I push the thought away.

Joy ties her brightly-colored shawl around her waist and continues the introduction. "Wonderful, welcome. We're so glad you found us, and we're excited for you to join the fun." She smiles as she makes eye contact one by one with each person who has their hand up. Kind of unnerving, but I'll take it.

"So, as you all know, this is the first of a four-week class. There's no pressure to come to all of them, though. We're here to paint, yes, but also to enjoy our time together." I see some smiles and nods around the room. If their main purpose is to get people to come to Sunday service, they don't show it.

After her introduction, Joy patiently guides us through basic color gradient exercises, which turns out to be more fun than it sounded. I haven't picked up a paintbrush—in real life, I mean—since high school, but it comes naturally to me. Joy walks around the room, giving encouragement and advice while retelling anecdotes about her decades-long career as an artist. It's really nice of her to donate her time to the church by teaching this class.

Across from me, a curly-haired thirtysomething man crouches down next to an adorable little boy. "Jesse, it looks like we don't have much red left. Try to leave some for everyone else, yeah? A little goes a long way." The son doesn't respond, but he obediently returns the bottle to the clear plastic bin.

Joy's hovering near our table now. I get the sense she's talking about me when she says to the room, "I know that basic technique work like this can be tedious, but try not to rush through it. I promise you, if you take your time with it, it'll pay off." I smile up at her without saying anything. If only she knew about my whirlwind adventures in the simulation, my pilgrimage toward optimization and efficiency.

"I have some of my pieces around the room to show you different examples of brushstrokes, if you're interested," she continues. "If you look carefully, you'll see that any beautiful masterpiece is made up of the same kinds of small strokes of color that each of you are making."

She shifts her gaze to the trio of fidgety toddlers in the corner, giving them a wink. "And tell you what, since it's our first day, I'm going to keep my lecturing portion short, and, instead, let you loose to practice your brushstrokes however you like." She presses a button on the '90s-era CD player, letting soft jazz piano music fill the room. The friendly murmur of conversation bumps up a notch.

I stay focused on my canvas. So far, I have six color gradients aligned in neat rows. The first ones I did are sloppier, but with practice I got the hang of how to keep my hand steady so that my brushstrokes come out cleaner and smoother. It's so nice to be able to work with my hands—I even got some paint on my them accidentally, which makes me feel like a real artist. But my goal isn't to become Picasso; my goal is to have painting as a self-care activity that I can escape to when I'm feeling bad. I think it's working.

"Whoa, they're so good!" a lanky teenage girl says to her friend next to her. I look over and see she's gesturing to Joy's large acrylic paintings propped up against the bookshelves along the wall. I set my paintbrush down. I can't agree more; even from where I'm sitting several feet away, it's wild how bold they seem, almost as if they were alive. I walk over to get a closer look.

They're all scenes based on Bible stories. Some of them I recognize instantly, while others take a moment to jog my memory. A sex worker pouring Dior perfume over the feet of a Jesus who actually looks Middle Eastern, a pregnant, modern-day refugee and her husband that allude to pregnant Mary and Joseph, a prodigal daughter returning to her mother's open arms. They're very progressive. I'm impressed.

Then, I'm startled by a low voice behind me. "Excuse me, is it…Erin?" I turn around to face a guy about my age, his hands resting casually in the front pockets of his blue jeans. "I don't think we've met, have we? I'm Joel, nice to meet you." We shake hands. He seems a vanilla kind of nice, but nice nonetheless.

I clear my throat. It always takes me a second to remember how to speak to someone new. "Hi, nice to meet you. How's it going? Admiring Joy's artwork?"

He nods, smiling with his dark-brown eyes. "How could I not?" He adds, "What do you think of them?"

"Hm, well they're...fresh? For lack of a better word. I mean, I like the mix of old stories and new ideas." I set my hands on my waist and look back at the paintings.

"Oh, absolutely. So, you're familiar with Bible stories, then?" he asks, raising his eyebrows.

"Yeah, watched a lot of *Veggie Tales*," I chuckle. "I grew up in the church, over in Pennsylvania. If I remember correctly, my Sunday school classroom was a lot like this one." I nod toward the wall of paper cutouts showing a group of racially diverse children sitting in a circle with Jesus while sheep graze the green field.

Wait, I don't want to give him the impression that I'm here for the church bit. "But if I'm being honest, what brought me here was the free painting class."

He runs his fingers through his straight black hair and laughs. He has a "fun uncle" vibe that reminds me of someone else, but I can't quite put my finger on who.

"And you? What brought you here?" I ask politely. I'm guessing he's a good churchgoer. His name is Joel, after all.

"Me? Nothing special. My parents used to come, and I guess I just never stopped coming." He shrugs and adds, in a stage-whisper, "I also just don't have much to do on weekends and I teach art, so this is a good way to get myself out of the house."

He teaches art? I don't think I know anyone who does that. So why does he seem so familiar to me?

I nod and share more about myself in return. "I kind of slipped away after college, but I used to really like coming to church. I work in tech now, or tech-adjacent academia, I guess." I picture my lab mates in their default states: Noah whispering thoughts and prayers to the voice recognition app on his smartwatch, Eleni and Julia chugging their meal replacement drinks in holy communion, Sean preaching the gospel of decentralized cryptocurrencies. "Sometimes tech feels like a religion in itself, honestly." Joel nods and we sit with that thought for a few beats.

"Would you ever consider coming to Sunday service? No pressure, it's just that there's a lot of techies in our congregation, so maybe you might have stuff in common with them," he suggests gently. Ah, there it is, the friendly evangelism.

Then suddenly, it hits me: Joel is like Jed, from the simulation! My entire body buzzes with energy and excitement, and I struggle to keep my cool. Jed taught pottery and was super sociable. But how could my neural net have generated a character based off someone I hadn't yet met? Alternatively, maybe Jed wasn't based off Joel, but rather Joel happens to resemble my ideal companion. I guess that's a sign that Joel's someone I should get to know better.

"Yeah. I definitely have thought about it before." I pause, trying to focus on the conversation and find the right words to explain my faith situation.

I clear my throat. "A couple years ago, when I'd just started my first software engineering internship, a senior engineer told me to be a louder presence in team meetings. I know he meant well, but something about it bugged me. It made me think of the Bible story where Elijah's standing at the edge of a cliff, listening for the voice of God—you know the one I'm talking about?" Joel nods. "I don't remember the details, but it was something like how he searched for it in the fire or some other kind of big flashy sign, but in the end, God was in the gentle whisper of the wind. The story reminded me that true power doesn't always look aggressive and stereotypically masculine. I crave more of that way of thinking, but I was never sure if church was the right place for me." I mean, did Ethel go to church? Definitely not.

I turn to Joel again, wanting to know more about his potential similarities to Jed. "But what about you? What do you like about coming here on Sundays?"

"I guess I like the gray areas of faith and truth, of it being okay to never really know what to think. Grappling with unanswerable questions and going on spiritual journeys with no definite destination." He makes sweeping hand gestures, half-jokingly. He's warm and welcoming, a natural conversationalist, like Jed was.

I nod. "I get that." I think I've been spending so much time at the lab that I forgot about any other way of thinking.

Like, at the lab, if you were one lost sheep but the other ninety-nine were still there, they would undoubtedly leave you. If you were a prodigal son, they wouldn't take you back after you squandered your inheritance—that's called a bad investment. Because we don't have time to waste, money to waste. Because that's how businesses succeed, how technological innovation thrives. Disruption, domination. Oppression, exploitation. We focus on the continuous accumulation of resources and knowledge. If we're not growing, we're shrinking, and if we're shrinking, we're dying. We got here and now we want to get there. We take ourselves so seriously.

Just then, a tall guy with a worried look on his face taps Joel on the shoulder. "Hey, sorry to interrupt, can I talk to you for a minute?" He glances toward the door, seeming impatient.

"Of course, yeah. And Erin, it was nice to meet you," Joel says, grinning at me on his way out the door.

"Yeah, no worries. Catch you later," I say as I head back to my seat, genuinely hoping to talk to him again. Inspired by this social interaction, I start a conversation with the father and daughter sitting on my left and for the rest of class, I paint up a storm.

When class ends and I step outside, I'm greeted by birds chirping and a wind chime ringing. It's nice and sunny, too, as if God himself were smiling down upon me. I feel like I'd been unconsciously clenching some invisible muscle and I'm just now starting to realize what it feels like to let go.

Satisfied, I take a deep breath. The algorithm really knew what I needed.

14

―――

A soothing acoustic guitar melody flows out of my nightstand speaker. The music would be nice, if it weren't for the fact that I've spent the past two hours like this, unable to fall asleep and instead lying wide awake in my bed.

"Deep Sleep," "Night Rain," "Sleepy Piano." I've tried all these sleep playlists over the past several weeks. Each have over one million likes and is supposedly scientifically proven to be effective in helping you fall asleep. Why don't they work for me?

I prop myself up on my elbows. "Hey Spotify, pause."

Kicking off my blanket, I roll over to the other side of my twin-size mattress. I wave my hand blindly above me until I find the switch to turn on my lamp. Warm light washes over the room, exposing its state of disarray; everything looks better in the dark. I stumble over to my desk in the corner, where my laptop is charging. I seize a stray scrunchie on the ground and tie my hair back; I'm a professional, even in bleary-eyed insomniac mode.

I let out a sigh, trying to get my frustration out of my system. Paint. I should paint; that's what Ethel would do.

Yesterday's class went well. Painting felt right; it felt like I found a home, more of myself, where I'm meant to be. Sitting in a room full of strangers has never really been my jam, but the painting itself was great. Tomorrow, first thing in the morning, I'll buy my own set of paints, brushes, and canvases. Where did Joy get the ones we used for class? I flip open my laptop and type out a reminder to ask her.

I glance at the week ahead on my calendar widget. I'm genuinely looking forward to next week's class, to seeing Joy's enthusiastic smile and chatting with Joel again. Getting to know the other folks, too. Everyone was so nice there, so welcoming. I could start coming on Sundays, even. It would give me another chance to make friends with everyone. Would they want to be friends with me? Maybe I'm getting ahead of myself. But Ethel had more friends than I do, so I probably need more friends. Really, I just have Abi, and we're not even that close anymore.

Logically, I know that this world isn't the same as—or at all similar to—the simulation, but even so, it turns out that some things carry over; the neural net's vision for my ideal creative hobby was pretty accurate. So why not try using Ethel as a blueprint to reinvent myself in other ways, too? There's open space on my calendar, light gray boxes of hours in between brightly colored scheduled events. I have my whole life ahead of me.

I'm young and free. I have big dreams, don't I? I close my eyes for a moment, concentrating. I don't know exactly what it is I want from my life, but I know it's more than this. So I might as well try getting what Ethel had; it can be another fun experiment, a part two.

But where to begin, to make my life like Ethel's? Let's start with physical health. I search, "meal prep easy healthy," "what vitamins should i take quiz," "how much water should i drink," "fitness trackers for beginners." I scan through the top hits from each query, bookmarking some for later, skimming product reviews, clicking links that link to more links. After those searches comes "how to feel more energized," "how to feel more motivated," "personal trainers near me." I create a new document and quickly fill the screen with a dozen bullet point notes.

And speaking of health, what about mental health? Self-care is so important, after all. In goes "therapists near me," "self-affirmations instagram empowering," "self-help books stress relief." Also, I think I need to find a new therapist, someone like Ren.

The cursor blinks steadily at me in the search bar, waiting for its next instruction. What else, what else can help me? What questions should I be asking but don't know to ask? That's where search suggestions come in. Related questions, yes please: "how to improve your friendships," "best minimalist home designs," "life hacks for productivity." More and more queries follow.

Two point eight million search results in 1/10 of a second, four point one million search results in 2/10 of a second; each search yields more than I can ever imagine. At first, all the hyperlinks are blue, but as I sift through them expertly and log them on a document stored in the cloud, they become an array of blue and purple, and then I'm on to the next query.

I imagine the five-core processor making sense of the letters I type onto the retina display, going byte by byte, commanding the flood of electrons to move, the semiconductors activate just so. Fiber optic cables running thousands of miles across the planet to get the world's data to my screen.

I started learning to type when I was seven, desperately wanting to have my poems printed in impeccable black letters. Ever since then, the keyboard and mouse have become extensions of my body. I am no longer merely mortal as I soar through the dark mode home page of Google, my ninety-words-per-minute typing speed like winged sandals. The thrill of being everywhere and knowing everything all at once.

The road to better focus, better sleep, and a better me is an aesthetic one. Sleek websites with a modern feel. Branding that evokes simplicity and transparency. Short, catchy tag lines in sans serif fonts against pastel-colored backgrounds. The intuitive interface guides me through each page, cheering me on with phrases like "you got this" and "almost there" as I go. And "have we mentioned there's a special sale happening now?"

Images of diverse models proclaim self-empowerment and urge me to join their community. It's the only intelligent, eco-friendly, socially conscious, and feminist thing to do. I'll start with a standing desk, an essential oil diffuser, a meal prep subscription, a home automation system, and an online data science class.

I review the shopping cart totals. It's a lot, but I'm worth it. I need it. I have better things to do, bigger and more consequential things to worry about. I wasn't born to cook meals, fill the gas tank, clean the house. I know my purpose; I'm not here to just maintain the world, but to transform it. I can't let anything hold me back. With each click of the big blue Submit Order buttons, I feel a hit of dopamine course through my veins.

Why didn't I do this sooner? Ethel wouldn't have needed to do any of this in the first place because the system would've already laid it out for her. Sighing, I shut the screen. Well, this is enough for tonight. It takes a minute for my eyes to readjust to the soft light in my room and for my heart rate to slow down.

As I roll back into bed and switch off the light, I hear Bruce snoring in the hallway. Lucky bastard, he'll never have to worry about trying this hard to be like his simulation counterpart, Buddy.

15

———

"It's terrifying," Joel says, mesmerized by the pottery works displayed on the shelves around the studio. He's standing alarmingly close to one fragile-looking painted clay vase. Is there something I missed, something more to look at? I stand closer to him and follow his gaze, but I'm still not as impressed as he is. He seems to be seeing so much more. Perceiving more. Is this how Jed looked at pottery in the simulation?

I chuckle and wait for him to say more. When he doesn't, I nudge him along with, "Why do you say that? Aren't they beautiful?"

"It's terrifyingly beautiful; with art, there's no set of answers, and the potential answers change depending on who you are and what state of mind you're in," he replies, turning to face me at our table. "Or maybe it's 'beautifully terrifying.'" He winks shamelessly, which kind of gets on my nerves, but I guess I've been looking for a change of pace and he's as good as any.

Tonight, Joel's clad in a navy-blue polo shirt and khaki pants, a thick denim jacket slung over the crook of his arm.

His frat boy look doesn't suit his sweet, almost childlike personality; put another way, it's off-brand. Meanwhile, I'm still in the black blouse and dark jeans I wore to work, since I came directly from the lab.

"Yeah, I get that." I come back to my seat, resting my elbows on the metal workstation and my head on my hands. "Art has always made me feel unmoored, but in a good way, I think." I always feel like the artist had one thing in mind when creating it, and I have my own set of thoughts and beliefs that makes my experience of the work necessarily different from that of the artist.

The Wednesday evening air is chilly in the high-ceilinged studio. I've gotten used to the smell of wet clay and paint, and the lo-fi beats permeating the space. I like that the place is reasonably clean and organized but not impeccable; there's an occasional fleck of paint or some other such stain on practically every surface. At the table next to us, a green-haired teenage boy coughs into his elbow and a tattooed older woman chats with a short, bearded man. Even the diverse group of people helps add to the ambience.

I'm usually exhausted after work, but I'm feeling energized, probably because of the newness of this place. I should try new things more often. I should hang out with Joel more often.

Last Saturday, after painting class, we went downtown to the modern art museum because I could not believe he hadn't been before. I was initially nervous about taking him because I'd only ever gone alone, the art—or rather, my experience of it—too personal to share with another human being. I thought the vulnerability was terrifying, but it turned out to be "beautifully terrifying" or "terrifyingly beautiful," using Joel's words.

We shared our take on the art, and he said he felt we were "kindred spirits," to which I rolled my eyes good-naturedly. We found out we're both pretty new to Los Angeles, and we share a guilty pleasure of overpriced coffee from mostly white and very hipster café joints. Overall, it felt nice to be able to show him around a place that felt like my second home, especially since I hadn't gotten around to visiting it in a while. We also made plans to try pottery at this studio because Joel knew a gal who could get us a discount.

I wave him back toward our table. "All right, come on, let's figure out what we want to make. I've been sitting here for almost half an hour, and I still have no idea." There are a couple other groups here, too. Two strong-armed women are throwing red clay onto a wheel. They seem to know exactly what they want to make, and I envy them.

"We could paint something? We don't have to make something from clay," Joel says, calmly walking back and settling into his seat across from me. He puts on the canvas apron slung over his chair, and I follow suit. "You know, Joy would be so proud of us for using our new skills." He ties the apron carefully around his waist and mirrors my posture, resting his elbows on the table and his head on his hands.

"Yeah, you're right. But we're at an actual studio, with a wheel and a kiln and other fancy tools that I don't even know the names of. I want to do something with them." I don't remember the last time I found myself in a pottery studio, and I don't know when the next time will be. Plus, there are some friendly-looking staff members floating around, supervising the place and helping newbies out. Like Jed from the simulation, I imagine.

"Do you *want* to?" Joel asks.

I pause. "Well, if you put it that way, I don't know. I'm honestly kind of tired."

"Then let's paint." He smiles. "Because what are we here for?" He pauses for effect. "Not to become potters—to enjoy ourselves!"

I laugh. "Sure. We can be like ten-year-olds at Petroglyph."

We head over to the section of prekilned pieces ready to be painted. There are a couple different options: mugs, plates, and bowls. Some of them are chipped or have random stray marks on them, but otherwise they seem to be in decent condition. I pick up one of each, carefully turning it over in my hands and considering its shape and heft.

The mug seems most practical since I want to drink more tea at home. It's also rife with creative possibilities, since it's a cylindrical shape with a curved oval jutting out from its side; an elephant's trunk, maybe? The outline of a human ear? The handle of a tote bag? I hold the mug I've chosen closer to my chest, feeling like I've established a bond with it.

Joel picks out a bowl and places it upside down on his head, like a hat. He giggles.

"Aren't you so funny?" I tease. If he had a bowl cut, this would be a glorious opportunity to make a joke, but his hair is buzzed such that none of it is visible, so he just looks like a mushroom. A trio of teenagers near us laugh along while they continue kneading their clay.

After taking our selections back to our table, we spend time looking over the paint rack, which holds dozens of different colors. "What are you going to paint?" I ask.

He replies, "Not sure yet. But I think I could do something with these colors." Joel reaches for a grayish blue, a mustard yellow, and a bright red orange. A nice palette. I keep standing before the giant rack of bottles, overwhelmed at the number of options. I can feel Joel silently looking at me for a few moments before quietly retreating to our table. For a few minutes, I stand there awkwardly, trying to brainstorm what to paint. I fold, taking out my phone and searching "color palettes for summer," "creative painted mugs," "cool clay painting techniques." I scroll swiftly through the image results, but I don't find anything that stands out to me.

I want my mug to look good. I want it to be special, special enough to remind me that I have had a fun time with a friend. I'm starting to sweat from the pressure, which is kind of a stupid reason to freak out, I know. Eventually, I decide to just go with an array of earth tones, reddish browns and grassy greens. What would Ethel have chosen?

When I come back to our table clutching my bottles of paint, Joel seems to be in his own world. He's engrossed in his plate, methodically using a thin paintbrush to make blue concentric circles around the center of the plate, like a bullseye. He looks up at me and smiles warmly. "Hey, you're back," he says in a sweet voice.

I get my paints set up in a row in front of me. I still don't know what I'm going to paint, so I lie back in my seat and cross my arms. Something will come to me. In the meantime, we can chat. "You bet. So, tell me something about yourself, Joel." I feel like I hardly know who he is.

He raises his eyebrows, wanting a more specific prompt. I'm not going to ask the dreaded "what do you do?" question; he's not that type of person, and I don't want to be. "Okay, fair enough. What's your favorite smell?" My go-to when it comes to icebreaker questions, it's a real crowd-pleaser. Still, I grab my bottle of tea and take a swig to hide my embarrassment; it makes me feel a little ditsy in this situation.

Joel chuckles and puts his paintbrush down. He looks up at the ceiling thoughtfully before answering. "Before I say it, don't freak out by my answer, okay? I promise I'm not crazy." I nod and keep sipping my tea to look natural and casual. "My favorite smell is...blood."

I spit out my tea and we both burst out laughing. I know him well enough to know that there's no way he's a cannibal, a vampire, or a serial killer, but still, *blood*?

I give him a look without saying anything. People sitting nearby smile in our direction, some shaking their heads at how easily amused we are.

I look down at our table. "Oh shit, I ruined our stuff!" My spit tea left a splash of light brown splattered down the left half of Joel's plate and a few droplets on the handle of my mug. "I'm so sorry. We could probably just paint over it?"

Joel takes it in stride. "No, I think I'll leave it. It makes a great story, you know?"

"Yeah, if you don't think about the fact that it's my saliva, it's not so bad. It makes a statement." I lean forward slightly, getting a closer look at his plate. "But what were you going to make? All those delicate blue circles."

"Just a plain blue plate," he replies, somewhat sheepishly.

Now, it's my time to raise my eyebrows. "So why didn't you use a bigger brush? And why'd you put such painstaking effort into making circular strokes like that?"

"Yeah, there are easier ways to end up with a blue plate. But that's not what I'm going for." He shrugs before adding, "If I wanted a really easy way to get a blue plate, I'd just buy one."

"I get that, it's all about the journey and stuff. But it won't show up, after you put it in the kiln. All that extra work you're doing," I say, keeping my tone neutral.

"Yeah, it won't. But I'll know, I'll remember. And you will, too," Joel replies, staring back at me intently. My mind immediately turns to Jed, who looked at me that exact same way, in the simulation. It's uncanny.

I wrinkle my nose. "So, if I may ask, why didn't you spend that same time and effort making some beautiful intricate design, with a lot of different patterns and colors? Something that would mean something to everyone, even people who don't know that you put so much extra work into it."

"I did think about that, yeah. But what if I like that it's only meaningful if you know the story behind it? Makes it more...what's the word?" He makes a fluttering hand gesture in the air.

"Exclusive?" I suggest, teasingly.

"Personal," he says thoughtfully.

What's the difference?

I look away and change the subject. "You know how some people, after they make their stuff, they don't come back to the studio to pick it up? Even if it's a really nice, finished piece." Joel nods. "Why do you think that is?"

"Well, anyone who comes here has money to burn, you know, the high studio fees and stuff. So they probably don't care about the money they spent to make the piece. Generally speaking, time is their most precious commodity, time and energy." Joel runs a hand through his hair, pensive. "So people who don't care about their creation probably didn't put in much time and energy to it, and that's why the piece doesn't mean anything and it's not valuable to them."

I nod. "I get that. Like you said, there's lots of easy ways to end up with a blue plate, but it matters *how* you get it. If you buy it from the store, it doesn't mean much, but if you paint it yourself in your own special way, it means everything to you."

I keep chewing on this thought. "What about in other aspects of life? Transportation, for instance—driving versus walking. Both methods of transportation give you the same end result: getting places. I drove myself here since it's much more convenient and reasonable to drive four miles than to walk four miles. But if instead of driving, I decided to put in the time and energy to walk, I think I'd feel a lot prouder of myself and it'd mean a lot more to me that I completed the trek. Because my car makes travel so much easier and faster, I don't feel as satisfied when I arrive at my destination."

On the table to our right, a man sets down a bright green reusable Whole Foods bag that catches my eye. "Or what about getting food? Grocery shopping versus growing your own food. If instead of going to the grocery store, I went through the trouble of starting a garden in my own backyard, I'd feel so much more connected with my food, and I'd feel like it's a lot more precious because I produced it myself."

I gesture toward Joel, whose brow is slightly furrowed in concentration as he continues listening to my TED Talk. "And social connection. If instead of connecting with people online, you go the more vulnerable route of physically reaching out to them, each interaction becomes that much more meaningful and special.

"But what do you think, about going the harder-but-more-satisfying route on all those things, those basic human needs? Would it make you feel like your whole life was being taken up by time-consuming, labor-intensive, mundane tasks, or would you no longer think those things are mundane anymore and they're actually worth the time and energy you put into them? Because the time and energy you put into them makes them more valuable." Is that circular logic? Maybe, but it makes sense to me.

"I honestly don't know," Joel replies, crossing his arms over his chest. "What do you think?"

At the table to our left, an older white woman's phone starts ringing very loudly. The interruption scatters my mind for a moment, but then I regain my train of thought.

"Well, there are totally valid reasons why we choose convenience—usually, in the name of practicality—but I think it's important to remember that at the same time, there is value in the cumbersome alternatives—it's just more of a slow burn. They're not obsolete; they still have value. In fact, they have a kind of value that sexy technological advancements don't."

We let that sit for a few moments. Joel bites his lower lip and then chimes in. "I've thought about something similar, actually, something along the lines of 'has humankind ever made *actual* progress?' Sometimes it seems like for every problem we solve, we cause additional issues. Have we actually become net positive, compared to the olden days?" I nod energetically, resonating with that.

I start thinking out loud, starting with the examples I just used for my rant. "Grocery stores and restaurants make it possible for us to eat virtually whatever we want whenever we want it, but that means we no longer have physical exercise built into our daily lives like hunter-gatherers did. We have new modes of transportation that efficiently get us from one place to another, but now we have to live with the risks of car accidents and plane crashes. Social media and dating apps make it easier for us to connect with people, but now we have private corporations controlling and profiting off our dwindling attention and our need for validation."

From the corner of my eye, I spot a couple of mid-twenties tech workers with down jackets emblazoned with company logos, people who were born after the dawn of the internet, who've never known anything else. People like me. People like Ethel. People who are "forward-thinking"—but who decided that "forward" was the best direction, and who decided which direction was "forward"?

Somewhere behind us, an older man sneezes aggressively, which brings a more extreme idea to mind. "What about modern medicine, even? It's great that the common cold is no longer a death sentence, but now we have overpopulation, and tied to that is the climate crisis. So, is modern medicine one of the causes of climate change?"

Joel laughs. "I could cancel you on Twitter for saying that. But I also don't know if I can say you're wrong."

"Well, I'm not saying we should just go back to becoming cave people. I don't know if I'd say that modern life is *worse* than ancient life. I don't think we have more problems or fewer problems than our ancestors did—we just have a different set of problems. And same goes with the good stuff."

Joel's about to say something when I realize that the people around us are all cleaning up and getting ready to leave. I grab my phone and check the time. "No way, it's already closing time. Can you believe it?" I have my paints and paintbrushes laid out in front of me, but my mug is exactly the way it was when I got it off the shelf: off-white with two unidentifiable gray marks on it.

I look up at Joel and our eyes meet. He's also been considering my blank mug. "You going to get that fired?" he asks.

"You bet," I reply, and this time I'm the one who winks playfully. "It doesn't look like much, but it means a lot to me."

16

Hello, hello! Good morning, my friends, I say telepathically to the family of dark-green turtles. They're going for a morning swim through the stream. Their petite hands and feet effortlessly scoop the water to propel themselves forward.

It's a Sunday morning, the start of a new week. I'm sitting on a wooden bench at the campus botanical garden, which I didn't even know we had until now, and only learned of thanks to some more Googling on my part. Six point four acres of plants from all over the world thrive here, along with several species of fish and turtles in the clear, freshwater stream. Joel would love this place; I might bring him sometime.

This is the last step of my new morning routine. I woke up at 5:30 a.m. as the sun rose behind the clouds. I washed up, prepped a fruit smoothie to-go, and jogged to this spot while listening to a self-affirmation podcaster say things like "you are confident" and "you are important" right into my ears. It's brilliant; I shake off all morning sleepiness both physically and mentally, all in a span of a half hour.

Speaking of which, according to my new Fitbit, I slept for exactly eight hours and seventeen minutes last night. Three full sleep cycles, better quality rest than ever before. The app says it's probably due to my increased activity levels, which, by the way, my personal records for weightlifting have gone from mediocre to astounding.

And I can tell that my mood has significantly improved; gone are my days of passive-aggressive "suggestions" for the strangers who get on my nerves, no more counterproductive days of being a rebel without a cause. I usually get sick when the seasons change, but now, my immune system is a fortress backed by vitamin C, zinc, copper, and other new supplements tailored to my diet and lifestyle.

As a light cool breeze rushes past me, I feel limitless. I've practically inhaled technical interview prep books and computer science textbooks. I've attended eight networking events in the past two months and have two job leads already. I can almost taste my new engineering career as Ethel had it. Of course, it won't be exactly the same, but it'll still be great.

I take a long drink of my green smoothie, feeling the nutrients sink into my body. It's a kind of high, to feel this clarity of purpose. To feel optimistic. Optimal.

Oh, and can I still relax? Absolutely. I have a new list of self-care strategies and a frictionless routine for winding down after work, the main one being painting miniature nature scenes on canvas—which by the way, I sell on Etsy for a pretty penny. It's mind-boggling how much my daily routine has transformed in the past several weeks. This is a big upgrade for me.

I pace through the garden, clearing my head from what happened at the house last night. Abi and I have been arguing more often, about anything and everything, it seems. She passive-aggressively pointed out that we hardly spend time together anymore, even though she knows I have a lot on my plate. Not to mention that whenever I open up to her about what's going on with me, whether it's the new improvements in my life or the steep learning curve that comes with them, she bristles; conversely, I'm not really interested in hearing about her schoolwork and her dating life, and I don't care enough to pretend to.

What's more is that whenever Abi comes home, she goes straight to her room instead of hanging out in the living room like she used to. Abi won't say this outright, but I can tell it's because she hates the way I've rearranged our living room to be more space-efficient and visually appealing—even though when I'd texted her about it beforehand, she'd reacted to my message with a thumbs-up.

What really gets me, though, is that she even mentioned something about my spending habits, what with the packages that have arrived at the house, like my Peloton stationary bike, ergonomic standing desk, temperature-regulating mattress, and professional-grade acrylic paint set. Sure, it's a lot of stuff, but since we are completely financially independent of each other, what does she care?

I brush my hand over a bush of ferns. I don't know why she kept bringing it up, as if she were trying to shame me. I'm happy this way, and I don't see what's wrong with that. I have poured all my time and energy into setting myself up for a high-paying job and I have no interest in denying myself the nice things that I deserve.

Yesterday, I talked it over with Zoey, my new therapist. She affirmed me in my decision to set up an emotional boundary between me and Abi because continuing to put my energy into that argument would only drain us both; if we're not going to agree on something, we might as well just agree to disagree.

But then, Zoey hit me with, "Why do you think you're reacting in this way? Could it be that some tiny part of you thinks that there's truth behind what Abi said?" I still remember how my face flushed with heat when she mentioned that. And that's how I knew it was true; yes, I think I felt defensive about spending all this money on myself because part of me doesn't feel right about it.

But isn't that because as a woman, especially an Asian woman, I've been conditioned to take up the least amount of space, to be selfless to the point of self-sacrifice? Isn't it feminist to believe in my own wants and needs, and to go after them? As if to prove a point to myself, I pick a yellow wildflower from the weeds to my left, lifting it up toward the sky and twirling it around with my fingers. *What is it? Why can't I indulge in small luxuries?* I ask it. They'll pay off in the end because the more I invest in myself, the more I'll be able to earn. I chug the rest of my smoothie.

Naturally, the flower doesn't respond. It's already getting wilted from my warm hand, so I step toward the stream and toss it. It floats for a few moments before disappearing under the surface, and that's when I notice my reflection staring back at me. A young woman decked out in Lululemon athletic gear, skin blemish-free and complexion glowing, hair well-groomed. She looks like every woman on any mainstream magazine (one of the models there for diversity, of course, but still a model). She looks as much like Ethel as I ever possibly could.

Before I can ponder on this any longer, my phone vibrates. It's my calendar notifying me that I have to get going so that I can get to work on time. Without skipping a beat, I start running back home.

17

———

A few weeks later, I find myself speeding through the street on a lime-colored electric scooter, my head exposed to the chilly morning fog. I think through my game plan. I need to make a good first impression. Andrew, a friend of a friend who I found on LinkedIn, is one of the senior software engineers of a grocery delivery app startup. He's offered to show me around the place so that I can "get a feel" for what it's like to work on the engineering team at a tech startup. It's far from being a formal interview, but maybe it could lead to one, if I seem smart and personable enough. At the very least, it's a way to meet people in the field, and as they say, "your network is your net worth."

As a recent grad who didn't major in computer science or even some sort of engineering, I don't have a lot of great options for breaking into the tech industry. But I have what it takes; I was a brilliant engineer in the virtual world, and I'll be just as stellar in the real world. Besides, degrees and credentials are so old-school. I know I can do the work, and it's just a matter of convincing the engineers and tech recruiters, too.

At the end of the block, I stop and press the yellow button to cross the street. The startup's office is near downtown, and from what I gathered on their website, it's in one of those WeWork coworking environments that have lots of open space, pristine floor-to-ceiling windows, lush indoor plants, fancy lighting fixtures, and brightly-painted murals on the walls. From what I could tell from the pictures, it's the workplace of my dreams, just like Ethel's. Who knows, if all goes well in the next couple of months, I could be calling it mine.

The streetlight changes, and I walk my scooter across the street. This is the first time I've taken one of these, and I think it's actually kind of fun; it's nice to try new things. Change is good. I pass by a pack of twentysomethings in casual attire, nodding and smiling in greeting.

I sigh. I mean, I do like my current job at the lab; I genuinely care about the work, I'm pretty good at it, it challenges me, and it pays the bills. I like collaborating with Julia and the rest of the lovely team. It's just that research and academia can move pretty slowly because of inconclusive data or soul-killing bureaucracy. There must be other opportunities I'm missing out on. And what was that one quote? "Good things fall apart so that better things can come together." So that's why I asked around: Anyone have any openings for interns or entry-level positions in software engineering? Anyone willing to give me advice on breaking into the tech industry? I want to see what's out there. Nothing to lose.

I've been on the job search and application grind for about a week now, and even though I know my efforts will pay off, I hate this entire process. In the simulation, none of this business existed because the system automatically assigned everyone to what they were best suited for. That saves an untold amount of time and energy, both on the applicant's part and on the employer's part. Was there even a true recruitment, people ops, or HR team in the simulation? I don't think so.

I get back on the scooter and rush past huge apartment complexes and bourgeois shops and cafés, doing my best to steer clear of the scampering squirrels and the deep cracks in the sidewalk. I'm almost there; I can see the top of the office building behind the trees. The more I think about it, the more I think the system was indeed correct that I'm really best suited for engineering. Solving the world's problems and making lives better in whatever way possible—that was what Ethel lived for.

I slow to a stop a few feet in front of the glass door to the lobby area. It almost feels like my entire life has led up to this stage: the job hunt. Not just any job hunt, but the one that is best for me. The one where my passions, abilities, and opportunities align like the stars.

I'm a little sweaty from the ride over here, but otherwise feeling good. I pull my phone out from the front pocket of my backpack and get the scooter situation squared away on the app. Looks like I have several notifications, too; let's knock them out.

First is a text from Abi. A long one, which can't be good. A brief skim gets me the idea that it has to do with Sofia, the new girl. I shoot her back, *Sorry, girl. I'm busy right now. Hang in there.* A heart emoji seems appropriate. Then, I reluctantly add, *We can talk tonight.*

Next is a text from Joel, inviting me to join him for lunch tomorrow at his favorite Mediterranean place downtown. I feel my face flush and without hesitation, I reply, *Yeah absolutely! Thanks for the invite.*

I hastily stick my phone back in my pocket and glance at my reflection as I push open the door, admiring my new pixie cut and cartilage ear piercing. I got myself a new look inspired by Ethel because once I saw her, I realized that I looked like some country bumpkin from the flyover state suburbs. If I'm going to become a badass Silicon Beach software engineer, I might as well look the part, too. I take a deep breath and step inside.

***

"So, we sublease eight rooms, including the main hall," Andrew explains, walking a few steps ahead while turning his head to look at me. He speaks with ease, as though this isn't the first time we've ever met, and his slight British accent makes everything he says seem smarter and more refined. I'm glad I did my homework of glancing through his LinkedIn, Facebook, Instagram, and Twitter profiles beforehand because we hardly spend time on introductions and small talk. I get the sense that he's already internet-stalked me, too; it's more efficient this way.

Andrew starts diving deep into the history of the company, expressing his fervent enthusiasm about it while keeping his masculine-coded cool. The round tortoise-shell glasses on his nose and expensive-looking black headphones around his neck give him a distinctly hipster techie vibe. As if on cue, he hypes up the growth of the startup, adding "But we're growing superfast! We just hired three more engineers last week." I try my best to match his excitement.

"So this is the main space, where most of the engineering and product team works. There aren't that many of us here right now because work hours are flexible. You know, just as long as the work gets done, you're good." A bunch of guys are scattered around the room, some at desks and others lying around on couches engrossed in their laptop screens. A small team is huddled around a projector in the corner. They all seem hyper-focused on their work, in a deep state of flow. I love that feeling.

Andrew steps away for a second to mention something to one of the guys sitting at a desk. I recognize him as Ben, the founder of the company. The alpha male, or rather, the alpha male of the alpha males. He carries himself with power and confidence, the kind that Ethel had. The kind that I want for myself.

Could I see myself working here? Being one of them? I take a better look around the room, not wanting to miss a single thing. On the wall to my left are photos of smiling faces toasting at a restaurant, reaching a breathtaking vista point on a hike, presenting at prestigious conferences like SXSW and CES. It looks like these folks have a lot of fun together: camping, board games, laser tag, movie nights, go-karting. I guess I always imagined that the tech worker's life would be a constant grind, but now that I think about it, this makes sense; if you want to work hard, you also have to play hard. That's what it was like in the simulation, too.

I must be staring too conspicuously because Andrew turns to me sheepishly and says, "Yeah, we're still pretty new, but we're planning on bigger team-building trips. Rumor has it that there'll be a ski trip this winter. Tahoe!"

I laugh. "No, of course. It looks like you have a lot of fun around here." The more I think about it, the more I know I could use some fun vacations. We certainly don't have this level of bonding at the lab.

Andrew continues explaining more about the company culture and the day-to-day happenings, eagerly answering each of my questions. He seems like he really believes in his work, abilities, and potential—and his energy is infectious. It's like everyone here has a crystal-clear image in their mind of what an up-and-coming startup should look like, and they're turning their blueprint into the real thing. Like me, Erin, realizing Ethel.

He ends the tour at a kitchen area, fully stocked with snacks and beverages. "But yeah, that's basically it. If you want anything to eat or drink, help yourself." He cracks open a can of La Croix and takes a swig of it. I open the fridge and grab a coconut water. Delicious.

Then, his Apple watch buzzes and lights up. He runs his hand through his blond-brown hair. "Sorry if I'm cutting this short, but there's an all-hands starting in five. I don't mean to rush you out, though. Feel free to hang around and explore some more if you want."

"Oh, no worries at all. Thanks so much again for taking the time, Andrew. Really appreciate it." I want to ask what the big meeting is about, but he's already making a beeline toward his desk, grabbing his laptop on the way to one of the conference rooms down the hall. Looking around, it looks like everyone is starting to trickle into the meeting.

A TV screen at the front of the room displays a color-coded calendar of the day's meetings and events. And yes, in fact, right now there is a thirty-minute training on "Growth Hacking." What does that even mean?

Soon after, I hear a male voice begin presenting in the conference room, and I casually shuffle around the desks until I find myself in front of Ben's iMac, which is still logged in. Tempting. I glance around to see if there are any stragglers left, but as far as I can tell, I'm alone.

I crouch down behind the ergonomic rolling chair and wiggle the mouse back and forth. The screen brightens and shows me a cluttered desktop and a toolbar at the bottom with the standard workplace apps. At first, I hesitate, but then I figure, why not? Knowledge is power. I probably won't find anything too interesting, anyway, but maybe I'll be able to get the inside scoop on what they're looking for in new hires, that sort of thing.

I glance through Ben's company email, calendar, and project management software, making sure to leave each one as I found it. It's pretty dry: quarterly fiscal reports, ideas for new markets, technical design reviews. But there's an itch in the back of my mind that keeps me looking for...something.

I open Slack and browse *#general*, *#random*, and some channels dedicated to specific projects. They're not very significant: *Here's our new org chart, Update on our competitors, Urgent technical issue re: new feature.* Message threads contain clarification questions and answers. Emoji reactions include the classic racially ambiguous thumbs-up as well as some custom-made company-specific ones. Most of the communication comes from the executive team, Michael, Ben, Will, James, Luke, Aaron. Profile pictures show them wearing their company shirts or jackets while mountain biking, beer brewing, and the like.

Their tone is colloquial, lots of *dude*s and *sick*s and even some *fuck yeah*s. From the timestamps, it looks like they're online at virtually all hours of the day and night. I keep scrolling. It's nice seeing this camaraderie. They're a tight-knit team, a really cool one at that. They seem to be close friends. Buddies.

But then, when I see a message from a certain Lauren, I realize what's been bugging me about this place.

***

Lauren's wearing a flower-patterned blouse in her profile picture. Her brown hair is long and wavy, and her makeup is bold. Her profile says she's on the product engineering team. I want to be happy to see a fellow "female engineer," as they say, but in the first split second of seeing her, all I can think is *Oh, she is a woman,* and I don't want to admit it, but there's a subtle discomfort that follows. Even though I also identify as a woman!

Not only that, but the way I initially reacted to Lauren, with a subtle aversion almost, that's how people must see me, too. I will always be seen first as the "the woman," whether consciously or subconsciously.

I refocus my eyes to stare at my faint reflection on the screen. I'm not even that much of an "other." I'm cisgender, straight, thin. I come from an upper middle-class family. I have no disabilities, whether visible or invisible. I'm a legal citizen of America and English is my first language. In so many ways, I am the normative identity.

Even so, I may never belong here in the way that I want to, in the way that Andrew does, because I don't fit in perfectly. I scroll through messages from other engineers on Slack, paying attention to their names and profile photos.

Michael, a white, broad-shouldered man, talks the most and is mentioned the most. His peers Claire and Rita hardly seem to exist. Dave's messages are stream of consciousness and shameless, but still appear to be well-received with rocket-launch emoji and praise-hands emoji; meanwhile, I can tell that Lauren's words are meticulously drafted before she hits send, and the few replies that she does get are short and stilted.

I didn't notice this before, but now that I see it, I can't unsee it.

The *#random* chat, for watercooler conversations, is almost entirely composed of men's names and stereotypically masculine activities. *You gotta watch the Dodgers game, At the gym and just benched 200, I fucked up my Ethereum wallet can anyone help.* The culture is homogeneous, defined by one very narrow demographic. And the thing about culture is that people naturally feel more comfortable around people who are similar to them. As a result, they work better together, which is better for the company's bottom line. *@Trevor @Max and me had this massive epiphany about this new feature while we were out for drinks last night. #TeamBonding am I right?*

I skim the private conversations between Ben and the other executives, about hiring. *Get the MIT grad. But is she any good? What's even on her github.* I cringe. What they see in people is their market value; what programming languages they know, where they've interned.

They're not interested in whether you have an understanding of what it's like to overcome trauma, what it's like to be stared at in public, what it's like to live in constant worry of not being able to pay rent. Aspects of selfhood that have inherent value, but that are difficult to describe, difficult to market. *Who cares man? We just need more good coders ASAP.*

It's not fair to spend more time training that one and we don't have time for that anyway. Tell you what—if Ava can keep up with the rest of the team, she can stay; if not, she'll leave. They believe in equality, not equity. They will invest the same amount of resources into everyone, even if you started with less. It wouldn't make economic sense to invest in someone who knows less, when there are others out there who already know enough. They have a system, and if you do not fit in it, they'll simply find someone else who does. *I mean sure, but she seems like no fun, not a good fit for the team.*

They see an investment in diversity and inclusion as a loss of potential profits. *We don't have time or money for that.* Even though increased diversity is statistically shown to produce increased profit in the long run. But I want to, I need to, work for a company that embraces diversity even if it doesn't increase profit, which is to say that it decreases profit. I want a company that invests in diversity simply because that's the right thing to do.

These people are blissfully unaware. They don't think twice about the opportunities and votes of confidence that are handed to them because they don't have to. I hate to admit it, but if I were them, I don't know if I would, either.

18

___

"I'm so glad you reached out, Erin, to move our appointment up. I do my best to be flexible for my clients because I know life doesn't just wait until the following week to punch us in the face, so to speak," Zoey says, settling her lean, five-foot-nine frame into her chair across from me. We chuckle. Zoey's a lot like Ren, my virtual therapist, in a lot of ways, which makes me think she's a keeper. She's young and relatable but also wise beyond her years, and she's very good at reading me. During last week's session, I told her everything about my simulation experiment and my vision for becoming Ethel in the real world and she seemed to understand. So, if this woman can't fix all my problems, I don't know who can.

"Yeah, thanks again for squeezing me in. I was really shaken after the job shadow day and I need some help," I reply. Zoey's not like Rachel, my old therapist; she won't just send me home with a generic journaling assignment or a list of miscellaneous self-care activities.

Zoey's office is furnished simply, with just a glass table between her chair and the client couch, a minimalist book-shelf in the corner. At the center of the table, a bouquet of yellow roses stands out beautifully from the navy-blue and tan hues of the room. On the wall to my left, two framed diplomas proudly display her master's degree in psychology and her license to practice therapy. It feels like a dentist's office, almost, but in a good way. I feel calmer just looking around the room. This is what therapy should feel like.

"Before we dive into it," Zoey says, "I was wondering if you'd tried talking about this job shadow experience with anyone else close to you? What about Abi? Joel? Anyone from your family, even?" Her piercing gaze kind of intimidates me, but I know I need that extra pressure.

I nod. "Yeah, I tried talking about it with Joel, and he was as supportive as he could be, but he doesn't really know what I'm going through because he's a far cry from the tech industry. I'm not entirely sure what he does for work, but it's something artsy." Reluctantly, I add, "As for Abi, I tried talking with her a little bit, but it wasn't going anywhere."

Zoey gives me a knowing look. She knows that one of my goals for therapy is to develop a stronger support system of people I can turn to when I'm feeling bad, and given that there aren't a lot of people in my life to begin with, I need to find as much support as I can from them. At least until I can find new people.

I inhale deeply, welcoming in the fresh lavender scent from Zoey's essential oil diffuser. "I know it just sounds like I'm making excuses, but since most of your clients are tech workers," I continue, "I felt like I had a good reason to wait until I could talk to you specifically."

I imagine Abi, in her default state at home, sitting cross-legged on the couch and munching noisily on veggie straws while Bruce snores fitfully next to her. Friday night, she'd asked me how it went, and I replied "Um, it was fine." I didn't want to talk about it with her and I knew that she knew that—and I knew that she knew that I knew that she knew that—but she still had the audacity to bring it up. Did she have nothing better to do? And then when I indulged her with more details about what bothered me about the bro culture, she hit me with something like, "You knew that already, didn't you? Gender biases and all that, especially in tech" and "Well, I guess that's just the way the cookie crumbles."

Zoey raises one eyebrow, as if to say that I'm off the hook for the Abi situation for now, but we'll come back to it later. "Well. At least we can rest easy knowing you tried. So, what is it about the startup shadowing experience that you'd like to focus on today?"

I thought about this on the drive here, so I'm all prepped and ready with my answer. "Ethel, my simulation self, loved her job and looked forward to going to the office every day. She really clicked with her coworkers, took pride in her work and felt that it was meaningful, and was in a constant state of learning and growing. She was an incredible problem solver and creative thinker."

I bite my lower lip, taking a moment to find the right words. "I wanted that, I still want that, so bad. But I don't think I can have that in the real world, at least not exactly, because here I'm reduced to my 'other' identities, as a woman in tech especially. I noticed it at the startup, and then I realized it's that way at my lab, too."

Zoey leans forward. "Tell me more, Erin. What's getting in the way of the life you want?"

"I mean, for one, there's the big glaring things like the gender wage gap and sexual harassment, which it seems like people are gaining awareness of, which is great. For me personally, I've been lucky enough to not run into those."

I stare at my hands folded neatly on my lap. "What bothers me are the small things that happen every day, the things I'm supposed to just deal with. Like when I don't get invited to informal get-togethers the guys are having, when people are dismissive of my ideas. Or the alternative, when people make a big deal out of "treating me like a lady" to "prove" they're not sexist. Sure, I can't prove they'd act differently toward me if I were a cis man because not everything is about gender et cetera, et cetera, but just because I can't prove it doesn't mean it can't be true."

"I'm so sorry to hear you're going through this, and this has been a fact of life you've had to get used to. I'm curious; what was it about your job shadowing experience that brought this up for you?"

"Yeah, so I was doing some sleuthing on one of their computers, just looking through company chat logs. There wasn't much of note." I pause, wanting to choose my words carefully. "But at some point, I happened across a woman's name and profile photo, and my brain did a split-second double take. I realized that I saw her as an 'other,' and after that, I couldn't be sure if my perception of her could remain untainted by this initial thought."

Did that make sense? I add, "I mean, I knew in my head, the facts and figures about unconscious gender bias, but I never had this kind of chance to participate, as an outside observer, in the unfiltered inner workings of tech startup culture."

"Of course. Many of my clients from underrepresented communities have told me of similar experiences, so you're definitely far from being alone in this feeling. And on top of that, I know how important it is for you to reach your potential as an engineer. Not to mention now that you've gotten a taste of your hypothetical perfect world through the simulation experiment, I'm sure the real world must seem even uglier than before."

I nod. Finally, someone who's speaking my language.

Zoey pauses, letting that sink in. "I'm wondering if you think there might be a way to reframe this completely valid thought. I don't mean to take away from the seriousness of the issue of bias and inequity—after all, the truth is that it exists in this day and age and we must work with it—but could there be any good that comes out of it? Is there some way we can take this negative input and create something positive with it?"

I lean back in the comfy blue couch and feel my muscles relax into the memory-foam cushions. "I can't really think of anything."

Zoey offers, "Well, let's think for a moment, what if the industry were just how you wanted it? Fair and equitable."

Easy enough to answer. "It'd be great. I'd probably be more advanced in my career, and I'd like it a lot more."

"Is there anything you can do to help make that world a reality?" I nod slowly. Of course, I can't fix the entire world, but I can do my part. She continues, "For example, have you looked into any networking events and mentorship programs for women in engineering? Whether to join them for your own benefit or lend them a hand to advance their cause, or both."

I stop nodding and shrug. "Yeah, I know, they do amazing work and they're great for some people. But for me, it's like, a matter of principle: why should women be expected to take on those additional commitments when the problem is not with us, but with the greater system and institution? Why does the industry think we need to change ourselves in order to succeed, instead of seeing that it needs to change its definition of success and the ways of getting there?"

Zoey's expression shifts and she quickly readapts to what I'm looking for. She surprises me when she says, "Did you know there have been research studies showing that the more prestigious a field becomes, the fewer women and minorities will be in it? And conversely, the more men a field has, the more prestigious it becomes." Part of me is mind-blown by that social science, but another part of me isn't surprised.

Honestly, I've probably heard research findings like this from other women in tech, but it's not the same unless you experience it and process the experience yourself.

I run my fingers through my hair. We're getting into it. "If you play by the rules that men play by, you get called bitchy; if you don't, you get blamed for being soft and quiet. So you need to seem confident and modest at the same time—how do you even do that? Not even that, how are you supposed to be confident in a place that tells you through every unspoken signal, or even spoken signals, too, that it has no confidence in you. And when you inevitably need help like anyone else would, people think it's proof that you're not smart enough, and you don't make the cut."

I take a breath. "Or they treat you like some kind of queen but like, a snow queen almost? Like they're afraid of being accused of being misogynist pigs, even though we all are because social conditioning et cetera, et cetera. What's even scarier is that on the surface, it's nice, to be so clearly and painfully respected. But it's like they're trying to overcompensate because women aren't naturally entitled to the same level of respect—I want a world where we wouldn't *need* to actively love and celebrate and affirm women, where it's something we just do naturally."

Zoey nods vigorously, encouraging me to continue. "Or they treat you like some sort of pet. They tease you and bring you along to stuff. It feels good, like you're *lucky* to be brought along with them and to feel included. But isn't that so…fucked? Why shouldn't *they* feel lucky to spend time with *me*?

"Or they treat you like their mom, like it's your responsibility to comfort them and sympathize with them. Supposed to be warm, caring, and approachable. And generally, I do like when people confide in me because it makes me feel special, but I hate when people act like they're entitled to my emotional energy.

"And the people with other minority identities, like black or Latinx folks, they're usually even less welcoming to me because they don't want to be associated more with 'others.' And who can blame them, right? They're usually too overwhelmed themselves trying to fit in."

We let that sit for a bit. Then, Zoey says, "It sounds like you have a lot to process."

"Yeah. The thing is, I just want to be seen as a normal person. To be a peer, an equal. Like how it was in the simulation, with my coworkers."

I shift in my seat. "Well, let me amend that statement. Yes, I want to fit in with the guys, but I don't want to become a female Jeff Bezos who makes it to the top through the same traditionally masculine tactics like individualism and competition. I want my femininity to be seen as valuable. I want to fit in with the group, but I want 'the group' to encompass those of all genders, you know?"

"Absolutely. We all want to be proud of our identities," Zoey replies.

Exactly. God, I love the sound of her voice, like bells tinkling.

I keep thinking aloud. "You know, sometimes I wonder, how much of my identity has been determined by society's gender biases, and how much of it is actually me? Can the two even be separated? Doesn't everyone wonder how their other-ness has held them back, who they would be without that social constraint?"

Zoey looks back at me and smiles. "Well. For you, we might have some version of an answer. Did the concept of gender exist in the optimized simulation?"

The question knocks my socks off. "I think so? But it wasn't something we put much thought into. We knew each other's pronouns and understood the differences between gender identity, expression, anatomical sex, and sexual and romantic attraction—and how these aspects varied a lot from person to person. It was normal to be different." I rack my brain, trying to remember what else. "Oh, and the system that controlled everything, the voice in my head, that was gender-neutral."

"I see. So, Erin, if you feel comfortable sharing, what was your gender in the simulation? Do you remember?"

"Well, I self-identified with she/her pronouns. I expressed pretty equally feminine and masculine traits. My body had female reproductive organs." Kind of interesting, now that I think about it.

"What do you think are the implications of that?" Zoey looks at me thoughtfully.

"Maybe my optimal gender is…woman? Or there was no optimal gender for the simulation world because there were no social biases, so it just kept the one I had in the real world?" I really have no clue.

Zoey narrows her eyes slightly, thinking. "Well, let's put it this way. If you had the option to wake up tomorrow as a cis white man, with all the privileges the world has to offer, would you take it?"

I have an immediate answer, but I pause for a minute because I want to think it through. It turns out that my thought-out answer is the same as my immediate one. "No, I wouldn't."

"And why's that?" Zoey asks, maintaining her poker-face expression.

"Because I want to know," I reply in a small voice, suddenly disarmed. "As much as I hate being an 'other,' since it's a burden on my own success and well-being, it comes with a silver lining: it gives me the push to try to empathize with people of other identities, people who I may never be able to relate to personally. It helps me understand that other people have completely different experiences of the world than I do, and that their experiences are just as valid as mine."

She smiles at me. I smile back, but a knot forms in my stomach. I know there's more I have to share.

"If I didn't have firsthand experience of what it's like being a woman in tech, and if I'd never cared enough to sit down and have an open-minded conversation with someone about this, I'd be pissed. I'd totally get it. I'd wish I were a woman.

"I might be a men's rights activist, what with all these talks that focus on women in the workplace but not on men. I might believe I rightfully deserve everything I have been given, that I am truly the genius that everyone has crowned me as in the false mirage of the meritocracy, that biology and evolution make this gender imbalance the natural and rightful order of things. Like that quote, 'To the privileged, equality feels like oppression.'"

I continue letting it all out. "Because as much as I actively try to work against it, I sometimes still see it in myself, too, with people who don't have the privileges I do. It's easier to talk to people who look like me. It's easier and it's faster when everyone has a common language and culture. I have to make a conscious effort to see Black people as just people, to see trans people as just people, to see disabled people as just people. I wouldn't feel as comfortable becoming friends with them; I would feel a small but unmistakable sense of awkwardness, discomfort, going against the grain."

I cringe. "I would feel like I'm doing some kind of charity work by interacting with them, being a good person."

"So, how do you feel about all this?" Zoey asks tenderly. "It's very different from your simulation world, isn't it?"

"Yeah. I have a lot to think about." I sigh. "I'll just keep doing the best that I can."

19

———

When I wake up the next morning, I lie in bed for a few minutes, staring up at the ceiling and snuggling my new weighted blanket up under my chin. I rub my eyes and pick up my phone to check my sleep score: eighty-eight, which is pretty good. I take a deep breath. I'm not just going to give up over this realization that the real world will only see me as an "other," that I will always have to prove myself. So what? I'm going to work with this.

I've come so far and I'm so close to becoming the new me, based on Ethel. I turn over onto my side and take in my refurnished and redecorated room. My standing desk holds books like *Zero to One*, *Getting Things Done*, *The Seven Habits of Highly Effective People*, and *Deep Work*. My house plants and my aroma diffuser boost my mood and productivity. My vision board makes me feel proud of myself for what I've already accomplished and keeps me motivated to pursue my next goals.

For the past four Saturdays, I've been going to painting class, but last week was the final session. This morning, I offered to go on a short hike with Abi, since the vibe between us has been tense and awkward at best, and she agreed. The last time we went out together was when we went thrift shopping for her date-night clothes—when she tried on a bunch of stuff but ended up hardly buying anything, by the way, so what was the point of that?

I sigh. I don't know exactly what I want to come from this, but I know something needs to change; I can't stand even being around her when I'm home. What should I say to her? *I'm sorry?* But what exactly did I do wrong? How do I not know what to say to someone I live with? We used to be two peas in a pod, and now we're each one pea in our own pod.

I get dressed in my Athleta sweatshirt and leggings, pop in my AirPods and try to pay attention to the Vox news podcast. I get out to the kitchen and make a fruit smoothie for both of us. I'll play it cool. A few minutes later, Abi emerges from her bedroom, Bruce slowly chugging along behind her. She was out late last night, not sure how late, but after midnight. She has bags under her eyes.

Abi opens the bottom cabinet and fills Bruce's food and water bowls before popping an instant oatmeal into the microwave. "Morning," I say, taking out an ear bud and trying to seem cheerful. Fake it until you make it, right? She nods at me and gives a weak smile.

"Hey," Abi responds, not taking her eyes off the microwave timer.

I pull out my phone and check the weather again. It'll be a cool and clear day, so if we're lucky, we might see some animals and nice leafage. I'm driving us to the local trail, which has pretty decent scenery and, more importantly, is only a fifteen-minute drive away. It won't be so bad, finally confronting the issue with Abi.

We eat our humble breakfasts in silence. I'm too nervous to offer her some of the smoothie, so I put the rest in the fridge. "Ready?" I ask, nodding toward the front door.

"Yeah," she replies. She bends down to pat Bruce's head. "Sorry we can't take you. It's too much walking." I'm not sure if we're going to walk that far, actually; I don't want to stay too long because I want to meet up with Joel later.

We put our stuff in my car and drive off. Abi fidgets with her seatbelt, seeming uncharacteristically unnerved—or am I just projecting? I turn on my music to fill the silence and some easygoing Vampire Weekend song comes on. Once we're out of our neighborhood and onto the highway, she gets the ball rolling.

"So, Erin. I know you've been going through a lot the past few months. I have, too." She leans back against the passenger seat. "I know I've brought this up before, but I think now we need to be more upfront about our friendship." She pauses. "What do you think?" For once, I'm glad I have to keep my eyes on the road—I couldn't bring myself to make eye contact with her.

"What do you mean, Abi?" I try to keep my voice clear and even. I can't tell if I'm ashamed of myself or mad at her. Maybe both.

"Are we still friends?"

The question feels like a punch in the gut. Why would someone ask that? How am I supposed to respond? "Of course we are." I reply softly. As if saying it would make it true, or at least make me believe it. Do I actually still care about Abi? The old me would say yes in a heartbeat, but the new me? I don't know.

"It hurts to see you every day but feel like I hardly know you." She gazes out the window, uncharacteristically distant.

"I thought we were friends, and I thought you would be here for me when I needed you. I guess I'm trying to ask if we could go through what we're going through, together."

"Abi…" I sigh. I would do anything to get out of this car, out of this situation. As we pass the exit that I take to go to the lab, I wonder, what if I showed her what I'd experienced? Would she understand me, then? Or would she hate me even more? What would she think of Aria? What would she think of Ethel?

She inhales sharply. "I can't keep going like this anymore, feeling like I'm pouring my energy into our friendship and getting nothing back from you. I need to know if I can depend on you for support, or if I need to shift my understanding of our relationship into being two random people who share the rent every month."

That's fair.

I think it's my cue to speak. "Abi, you absolutely have a right to stop being my friend, and I understand that you have valid reasons why you might choose to do so." My hands shake slightly as I signal rightward to exit. I don't think she meets my needs anymore, and I can't, or don't want to, meet hers. I can't think of a reason why I should invest energy into our friendship.

But part of me still wants to, or still wants me to want to, be friends with her.

I stop at the red light. "I'm sorry. I didn't know how much I was letting you down. I don't have a valid excuse; I've just been busy, and the startup shadowing ended up being shit." I cringe at how lame that sounds. "I didn't tell you this before because I knew you'd think it was stupid, but I think in the simulation, there was someone based off you. Her name was Aria. Aria was my best friend, but she was different from you in a lot of ways. I think she's more like what I'm looking for in a friend."

"Why didn't you tell me about any of that?" Abi asks in a coolly respectful voice.

"I don't know. I guess I didn't think you'd understand." The light switches to green and I turn left.

"I might not have at first, but you could've tried explaining it to me. Honestly, it feels like this vision you have for your new life is one that doesn't include me in it because, I don't know; I'm not worth it to you."

She really just said it. I feel myself immediately get defensive, and that's how I can tell that part of me knows it's true.

She used to be important to me, but not anymore. But why does part of me still wish she were? I don't know what to think or feel, much less what to say. I clutch the steering wheel tightly, my knuckles turning white.

We're quiet for the next few minutes, staring at the urban streets through the window. Abi brushes her fingers through her hair, fiddling with the ends. "To me, the value of a friendship, of any interpersonal relationship, doesn't come from the two people being on the same page and being perfectly compatible and everything coming easily to them; it comes from them having difficulties but despite those difficulties, caring enough about each other to work through them. To me, it seems like you don't want to put in either of those things."

"I don't know what to say, Abi. I had other things on my mind. I'm sorry I'm a bad friend." I wish I were stunned, but the truth is, I'm not; I saw this coming and yet I didn't lift a finger to fix it.

"Do you want to start putting in the work to improve our friendship, or do we need to end it?"

I open my mouth, but I can't speak. I feel so emotionally drained. We reach the trail parking lot, and I find a spot that's magically vacant. Two dads and their daughter are wrapping up a meal at the picnic tables in front of us.

My muscles are tense. "What would be your choice?" I ask, putting the car into park. I don't want to make this decision and I don't want to be held responsible for it.

"To stop," she replies flatly.

Of course. I can't decide whether I'm relieved to hear this or saddened by it. Objectively, I lost nothing, but why does it still hurt?

"Okay," I say restarting the car and shifting into reverse. I look in the rearview. "I'll take us back home." I should just cut my losses, but I can't help but add, "There's some fruit smoothie for you in the fridge."

20

Hello again, God! It's been a while, I think to myself as I slip into one of the wooden pews toward the back of the sanctuary. It's my first time at First Congregational's Sunday service, but the church-y vibe is familiar to me. At the front wall, church organ pipes flank a giant wooden cross. Sunlight streams in through the stained-glass window, making an aesthetically pleasing light effect. Above me, arched wooden beams support the high ceiling. It's designed to make you feel in awe of the presence of God, and it works.

Now, I know that Christianity wasn't part of Ethel's life at all—I mean, if there were anything like religion in the simulation, it'd be the technology, the system, that voice in Ethel's head. Regardless, I get the sense that going to church is what Ethel would do, or what the system would tell Ethel to do, if she were in my shoes because the past week has been really rough. It'll be good for me to surround myself with community. To return to a ritual, albeit one that I haven't practiced in years. To enjoy a change of scenery. To partake in some kind of celebration, never mind what it's for and whether I believe in it.

An older woman walks up to the grand piano on the stage and starts playing a tender and relaxing piece. We have about ten minutes before service starts and people are just starting to trickle in. I wanted to get here early to scope out the place. Toward the front, I spot Joy, the painting teacher, with what must be her two young daughters chatting together in their matching flower dresses. It's nice to see her again.

The stage is also stocked with a few guitars, a drum set, and some mics, all of which have seen better days. This facility has been around probably since before my parents were born, so it makes sense that a lot of the equipment, like the sound system and the lights, are insanely outdated. I can definitely see how the place could be revamped, like I did with my room.

But I think there's something to say about old things. It makes the place feel more like home, more personal, lived-in. The thing about replacing old items with the latest gadget is that you lose its personality, its story. Doesn't that count for something? Doesn't that matter?

Behind the music equipment are three rows of blue chairs, for the church choir most likely. There's a projector on each side of the stage announcing "Happy Easter" in big block letters to the congregation. Bouquets of flowers are arranged beautifully along the front of the stage, something special for Easter I assume.

The church doesn't feel like anything special, but I look for something about it that'll lift my spirits. There's got to be a reason why religious folks are happier and live longer than their nonbelieving counterparts. What better day than Easter to find out what all the hype is about?

I try to find a comfortable position in my seat, but the cushion is too firm. Feeling restless with seven minutes left before go-time, I glance through the shelf attached on the back of the pew in front of me, where they keep standard hardcover Bibles and red hymnals, along with the offering envelopes and cheap ballpoint pens. I pick up a Bible and flip through it slowly. Its inconvenient heft and its well-worn pages feel so reassuring in my hands.

It's not like I have anything better to do on Easter morning, anyway. I'm trying to minimize the amount of time I spend at home ever since I burned the bridge with Abi. I also need to take a break from my lab and my job search. I need to zoom out a bit, get some perspective.

I put the Bible back and place my hands in my lap, interlacing my fingers as if in prayer. I'm wearing my knee-length flower-printed dress for the occasion. Because it's fun to get all snazzy once in a while, to take a break from the "I don't care about how I look" style of the lab, drawn from the Silicon Valley tech startup influencers. Taking the extra time and effort to prepare yourself—even if it's by doing something as superficial as changing your appearance—makes whatever you do feel more special, sacred, or dare I say, holy. Especially because it really is a big day, Easter, the resurrection of Jesus.

I read through the church bulletin pamphlet that I picked up at the entrance. The announcements section says that after the service, there will be an Easter egg hunt for the kids and a photo booth along with a potluck lunch on the garden patio. I might stay a bit for that, just because it must be so cute to watch seven-year-olds frolic around. But part of me wants more, to see myself fitting in here, belonging as a member of the church family. In the simulation, I felt like I had a community, and I want that in the real world, too. I close my eyes and take a few deep breaths.

When I look up again, I'm surprised to see several dozen people throughout the pews. Everyone seems so content with their families and friends. Joel should be coming soon; given that he's the one who kept urging me to come, he'd better show up. I check my phone, but I don't see a text from him. He might be on ushering duty. I wouldn't have seen him on my way in because I took the side entrance, to help with my nerves about coming here for the first time.

"Hey, you made it!" I hear Joel's voice behind me. Speak of the devil! I feel a tap on my right shoulder, and, knowing he's probably on my opposite side, wanting to trick me, I turn back toward my left.

"There you are! Happy Easter," I reply, relieved to not be a loner anymore. He looks spiffy, too, in a white button-down and navy-blue chinos. "Service is about to start, isn't it?" Joel nods and takes a seat next to me.

The piano music fades away, and a tall blonde woman walks up to the podium. She adjusts the mic and greets the congregation with, "Welcome, everyone, to our very special Easter Sunday worship. Please join me in opening prayer."

I close my eyes and bow my head, like everyone else, and manage not to catch on fire for my lack of faith. The next few items in the service go by unremarkably: opening praise (singing and clapping to contemporary Christian praise songs), sharing the peace of Christ (greeting people I'll probably never see again), offering (giving money to the church because not even Jesus stands above capitalism).

Then, an older woman in a religious-looking robe thing comes onto the stage. "Good morning, we're so glad you could join us today. Happy Easter!" Her stole has really intricate and colorful embroidery. "My name is Pastor Kathy and

I want to give you a warm welcome to First Congregational Church. If it's your first time here..." She gives the spiel. After that, a pasty-looking teenage boy comes up to the podium to lead the scripture reading. His voice shakes as he reads a chapter from the book of Luke. Sweat stains show through his blue shirt, and I can't help but think it's endearing, the sense of reverence he has for this job, almost like he doesn't feel worthy to do it. It's in many ways the complete opposite of the technical presentations and product pitches that I'm used to at the lab, where you're supposed to impress everyone with your confidence that borders arrogance and your technical prowess that nears obsession.

As Pastor Kathy begins her sermon, I come up with a list of similarities between God and the simulation's system: they work in mysterious ways, they're all-knowing and all-powerful, they created and (to some extent) control the actors and the events that occur in the world, you have two-way communication with them, they're generally seen as benevolent entities that want the best for you. That's quite a lot.

Suddenly, Joel taps me on the shoulder. He looks like he's about to cry but before I can say anything he leans toward me and whispers into my ear, "I'm going to step out for a little walk, okay?" I nod but can't hide my concern. I start to stand, offering to go with him to keep him company, but he shakes his head and exits quietly from the outer end of the pew.

By the end of service, he still hasn't come back. I try texting him, but he doesn't respond. Right when I'm about to call him, a pair of police officers show up in the church courtyard. And that's when I realize something has happened, something the simulation would never have allowed to happen. But apparently God did.

21

___

"I know this must be such a difficult time, Erin. How have you been?" Zoey says delicately in her silvery voice. I feel the corners of my mouth start to curl into a sad smile, but then I completely lose it. Joel got hit by a car on Easter and he didn't make it.

"I don't know..." It takes me some time to pull myself together. "I mean, the irony is brutal. On the day we celebrate the son of God coming back to life, one of my closest friends *dies*! What kind of god does that to someone you care so much about?" I wipe my tears away with the back of my sleeve to dry my face, but they just keep coming.

I can't help but think that in the simulation world, he wouldn't have died—he means too much to me. He would've stayed in the church. In the simulation, even if he decided to step out, he wouldn't have gotten hit by a car because car accidents didn't even exist.

"It was so out of the blue! I don't even know the specifics of what happened because they wanted to respect his family's privacy, but from what I heard, it was just some idiot teenager, probably driving under the influence. Who does that on a Sunday morning? On *Easter*."

Zoey nods solemnly. "Do you have any insight into why Joel left the service in the first place? You mentioned he didn't seem well."

"Well, I asked around to see if anyone in the congregation knew why he'd suddenly stepped out of the service like that, but I didn't get any real answers. It seems like he was going through some mental health issues but never told anyone about what he was going through, and for some reason, he started falling apart that day." I rub my face with my hands. "I know it doesn't make sense to blame myself, but I should've gone with him. I could've been there for him, done *something* to save him, anything."

I try to even out my breathing, to slow down. "What I really want to say is that it hurts so bad to…lose someone."

"Of course. I know Joel was someone whom you were starting to feel close with, and that kind of relationship was something you'd been trying to find for a long time. And to have that suddenly torn away from you, that's a lot to go through." She looks at me tenderly, anticipating that I have more to say. I have so much to say, but I don't know how to say it.

I clear my throat and tell her about the memory I can't stop thinking about. "There was this park near UCLA that we used to go to. I'd bring a big picnic blanket and we'd lie down on it, spending hours watching dogs playing together. Yesterday, I went there for the first time since he died. I don't know why; I think I'd been feeling numb about all this, and I wanted to feel…something." I purse my lips, trying to collect myself. "But the moment I lay down, I realized my mind went automatically to wondering when he would come. I kept looking around, expecting to spot him among the passersby. At any moment, I'd feel a tap on my shoulder and there he'd be, grinning… I guess that's when it really hit me, what it means that he's gone."

Crossing my arms over my chest, I continue, "I think I really cared about him—I still do care about him. But I guess they're right when they say that sometimes you don't realize what you have until it's gone. I know it's cliché and I've heard it over and over again, but… I don't know." I grab onto a soft blue cushion and hug it on my lap. Zoey nods, affirming me like a mother would.

We sit together in silence for a few minutes, letting my grief fill the space between us. "So Erin, if you feel ready for it, there's a question I want to pose to you. You don't have to answer it now if you don't feel ready, but I wonder if it could be helpful to think about: what would you do if Joel were still alive?"

It's a seemingly obvious question, but it takes me some time to formulate my answer. I feel like there's so much; I don't know where to start. I stare at the leafy plant on the table, nourished by the afternoon sun pouring in through the window. "Well, I wish…I wish I'd spent more time with him. When we met, I'd gotten caught up in my stupid…obsession with changing my life. So I guess…I'd invite him to hang out more and accept more of his invitations to stuff."

"I think that's a totally valid answer," Zoey replies. "I'm wondering though, is there any way we can give Past Erin some grace? Do you think we could forgive her for not prioritizing time with Joel as much as you wish she had?"

I nod and croak out, "Past Erin didn't know what I know now. She was doing her best with what she knew at the time." *But it wasn't enough*, I want to add.

"And do you think Past Erin does deserve *some* credit because she did spend some time with Joel, even if it was not all that you wanted?"

I nod, sniffling. "Yeah, I know, but what really hurts is that Past Erin only spent time with Joel when it wasn't too much trouble. When I had leftover time, nothing better to do. And this sounds so bad, but...when I had some reason why I could justify spending time with him. Even though I wanted to—I wanted to spend time with him every day." Zoey raises her eyebrows, prompting me to tell her more.

The thoughts garbled in my mind come crashing out of me. "Like, I only felt like I could allow myself to spend time with him if it was 'quality time,' if there was some fun activity to do together that I did or wanted to do anyway, like the pottery class, dog watching, going out to eat.

"You know, before the simulation ended so abruptly, it was going to make Ethel start dating this guy named Jed. And when I first met Joel, the only reason I felt drawn to him is because he reminded me a lot of Jed. It was like the simulation 'endorsed' me spending time with Joel. Not only that, but...I think I only saw Joel how the simulation would see him: in terms of how much value he provided to my life, like how much fun I had when I was with him or whatever."

All that the simulation cared about was optimizing Ethel's ability to do work and reach her, my, potential; it didn't see any value in the overwhelming and inconvenient feeling of caring for people simply for its own sake. Maybe that's why I never picked up on how he might be struggling emotionally.

Zoey replies, "I understand; it sounds like you're feeling deep regret, which is so painful. I wonder if we could find more empathy for Past Erin; why might she have thought that 'wanting to' wasn't reason enough when it came to spending time with Joel?"

I close my eyes for a minute, thinking. "In the moment, I thought I'd be betraying myself by spending more time with him than I needed to fulfill my need for social connection or whatever. But now I realize that by sticking by this idea of the person I wanted to become, I betrayed the person I already was in that moment."

I roll up my sleeve, now wet with tears. "He tried to tell me, in his own subtle way, to ask me whether I might be running away from my feelings and from myself. I didn't get it then, but now I do."

"I'm so sorry to hear that, Erin. I can see you're going through a lot."

I get into another fit of tears. "There's so much I wish I could've told him, if he were still here." It feels like I'm opening a wound that's already bleeding.

"Okay. I know this will be difficult, but I'm wondering if you might find something in it for you. Would you be up for the empty chair exercise?" She gets the small chair in the corner and sets it down in front of me. It's a basic wooden chair, nothing special. I imagine Joel sitting there, leaning forward with a glint in his eye, resting his elbows on his knees and his head on his elbows. My imagination is so vivid it hurts.

I'm at loss for words. I look at the chair, then back at Zoey, then back at the chair. She looks back at me encouragingly. If I weren't feeling so shattered on the inside, I would feel silly for talking to empty air. "I...hey." I take a few deep breaths, laughing at how badly I wanted to have another shot at talking with him again.

It takes me several minutes before I find the strength to speak, my voice hoarse from crying. "I don't want to lose you because you…because you're really important to me. You mean a lot to me. I'm sorry it took me this long to figure that out. Can we hang out more, like you've been saying?"

I imagine Joel asking me why I changed my mind, and I respond. "In ten years, when I look back at this time, I want to know that I made some mistake at work because I stayed up all night talking to you about nothing and everything, I forgot my doctor's appointment because I was so fully present with you when you needed my support, I took a day off from my stupid nutrition plan so I could eat pizza and ice cream with you, I went to see a documentary I wasn't interested in just because I wanted to be there with you…" I close my eyes for a moment.

"Because I think, in some backward and inside-out way, the moments that really matter, the ones that I'll carry in my heart, are the ones that made me take a breath from my daily life, from my daily pursuit of becoming someone who would matter to the world—from this life I was so proud of." From the edge of my blurry vision, I can see Zoey nodding gently.

I keep pushing. "I had this idea that if I didn't chase after my optimal life all the time, it would pass me by, and I'd never get another shot at it; every single misstep took me further away from it. On the other hand, with people…well, they'll come and go. And I know this sounds really bad, but I figured I'd always find new ones who'd bring me connection and joy. And I still think that's true, I will probably find someone else someday."

I wipe my tears with my already damp sleeve. "But—but it'll never be *you*, the you who you are right now, and me, the me who I am right now. It'll never be *this* again. The world is a place of abundance and I know intellectually that I'll find something as meaningful, as fulfilling, as intimate, as what we were starting to have together—or maybe even more—but there's just something *else* about things that are as special as this. Like, I'll be able to find someone else who is special for exactly the same reasons you were special to me, but I—I don't know. It won't be the same." I look at Zoey, who keeps nodding.

I stare at the painfully empty chair. "I'm going to miss you so, so much." I look at Zoey and give her a nod, signaling I'm done. She moves the chair back and waits for me to transition myself back to the therapy session.

"Erin, I'm really proud of you for finding the courage to dig that deeply into your thoughts and feelings. How did it feel for you?" She smiles kindly with her perfect white teeth, like I imagine an elementary school teacher would. It's so comforting to be treated with the kind of care that little kids take for granted.

"Um, well, it…it hurt. Because what we had was so good, and now it's gone." I'm exhausted from all the crying and talking, exhausted by my own feelings. Usually, Zoey tells me how to reframe my thoughts and feelings into more positive and helpful ones, but how the fuck am I supposed to do that?

Then, Zoey does it for me. "Erin, I know that this hurt, this pain, is so much to bear. My hope for you is that someday, you can find it in yourself to be able to think of it this way: 'how amazing is it that I could feel so close to someone and that they could mean this much to me, that their absence could make me feel this way?'"

I burst into tears again. The immense amount of pain I feel now is a testament to the immense amount of joy we experienced together—and nothing can take that away from me.

Zoey's the perfect therapist for me, but even so, she can't bring Joel back.

22

Aimlessness. It's been two weeks of aimlessness. I stare at our sleepy neighborhood, holding Bruce's ratty old leash in my hand. He's meandering around on our doorstep, lethargic as ever.

Up until now, it was fine. Not having Abi, sure. Not being able to have the kind of job I wanted in the exact way that I wanted it, sure. I can deal with that. But having the one person I wanted to be close with become worm food six feet underground, the one person who actually resembled their counterpart in the simulation, that's too much. Is he in "a better place," as they say? Is he really?

I bend down to tie my left shoe, amazed at how much effort this takes me. Lately, in accordance with Zoey's advice, I've been doing the absolute minimum to get myself to the next day. I've been going to bed, but hardly making an effort to get a good night's sleep anymore, getting four hours a night at most. I have been eating most meals, but it's mostly fast food or takeout and I can feel my muscles atrophying from of lack of exercise. I give myself free time, but I spend it in a well of self-pity.

The worst, though, is my situation at the lab. I've been going to work, but whether I've been getting any work done is a different story. I missed the past two paper submission deadlines, first because I was so single-mindedly focused on landing an engineering job and now because things have been falling apart. I've felt a weird vibe from all my lab mates and I wouldn't be surprised if Julia straight-up fires me.

I pull the loops tight into a lopsided bow and begin tying my right shoe. I've tried to piece myself back together. I've thought about going to church, but that reminds me of Joel. They had his funeral Wednesday evening, but I didn't go because I just couldn't. I regret not going.

Even painting doesn't do it for me anymore. Maybe I'm different now, different from the person for whom I sent data to my software program, and now the things that worked for that version of me no longer work for me now. Does anything still work for me? It's like immediately after the simulation, I started evolving, and now I'm devolving back to my original state or worse.

This morning, I volunteered to walk Bruce, in a feeble attempt to make things up to Abi. It didn't occur to me that he probably doesn't like me, not like I ever went out of my way to be mean to him, but I don't coddle him like Abi does. But he doesn't have a choice. I lightly tug his leash and we start walking toward the park closest to our house.

I can't believe how different time feels to me. Before Joel died, I'd wanted to seize every moment and to not miss a single thing; now, I just want the day to be over. Better yet, I want this all to be fake. I stupidly look for signs that this world is just another simulation, that once I fail its test, I will return to the world where I actually belong. Maybe after I hit rock bottom, I'll realize this was just a bad dream.

Bruce randomly stops walking and whimpers at me. I sigh and crouch down next to him on the cracked and gum-ridden sidewalk. "What's wrong, buddy? We're just going for a walk on this nice day." With some ash and haze from the wildfires, a California classic. I stroke his grizzled head. "You tired already? We've only gone like two blocks," I add, being generous with my estimate of our distance. I don't know how long his walks are supposed to be, but I figure at least thirty minutes or so. Besides, shouldn't he be excited to go play outside?

We continue on our way. Soon, I hear a bunch of kids running around the playground. The kids seem fine, full of energy and excitement, but the playground has definitely seen better days. The green slide is tagged with graffiti, and not the artistic kind. The metal chains holding up the swings are brown with rust. Every flat surface is spotted with bird poop and the occasional piece of litter. I have no idea how often they clean this place, who does it, or how much they get paid, but I salute them.

Bruce and I settle down in a shady spot on the weedy grass behind the playground, facing the brown monkey bars. I think it'd be good for me to watch kids frolicking; I might learn a thing or two from them. But I should've brought a towel to sit on.

The dog's deep-set brown eyes stare at two preteen girls passing a frisbee back and forth, then he loses interest and rolls onto his back, expecting a belly rub. For a few moments, I glare at him in silent refusal. Why is this dog more high-maintenance than most humans I know?

I can't help but crack a smile. "Fine, fine." His fur is unpleasantly coarse, and after a few minutes, I realize I feel bad for poor Bruce, actually. It's not his fault that he's perpetually ill and only getting more senile by the day. Isn't he just doing his best, like the rest of us? He'll never come close to being like Buddy, my simulation dog. Just like how I'll never come close to being like Ethel. I sigh. "Hey, come on. Let's get you some water. Abi's going to be mad if you're dehydrated."

I force myself to stand up and lead him toward the sketchy-looking water fountain, which fortunately has a built-in dog bowl and a spout on the bottom. I fill the dog bowl with some clean-enough looking water and watch him lap it up.

Just when I'm about to drink from the water fountain for humans, I hear muffled sobs coming from somewhere around the corner, behind a huge gray shipping container. It's not a wail of pain and sorrow, but it's almost worse. It sounds like when you've been crying your heart out for hours and now your last remaining tears are squeezing themselves out. Because that's just what you do when it turns out that everything you've been seeking and striving for doesn't amount to anything at all.

At first, I keep slurping up the stream of water. Hopefully the crier's friend, sibling, parent, or guardian is on the way. But I have a feeling that's not happening. I glance around the vicinity, but I don't see anyone I could enlist for help; everyone's preoccupied with their intense game of tag or absorbed by their phone screen.

I've never been good with kids—I wasn't even good at being a kid—but you figure, I'm an adult now. There must be something I can do to help, if only to present myself as an authority figure and provide that false sense of security that gets kids through childhood. I've been in therapy; I must have learned something when it comes to how to help.

Behind me, Bruce gulps down water, seeming somewhat content even with his snout and chin hairs dripping wet. I crouch down to look him in the eye. "I'm a big girl, right Bruce?" His eyes seem glassy, like he didn't even register that I said anything. He probably didn't. After a pause, I reply to myself, "Yeah, I am. Let's go."

Together, we head toward the crier. And sure enough, looking very alone with the empty basketball blacktop stretching before her, sits a little girl with her back against the shipping crate, knees pulled up to her chest, head on her arms. I can't see the kid very well from here, but my guess is she's seven or eight years old. If I'd thought I had some clue of what to say, I've lost it all.

I don't move from where I am, several yards away from her. She's gone quiet now, and her body seems completely still. Is she even breathing? I clear my throat. "Um, hey, are you okay?"

She looks up at me, seemingly unsurprised to see a hot mess of a stranger with an elderly dog talking to her. Why do I feel like I'm more afraid of her than she is of me?

"No," she replies. Her voice is so...childlike. It throws me off for a second. I stand still, waiting for more, but she closes her eyes and hides her head in her arms again. What could it be? She's getting bullied at school? Her pet dog or cat or rabbit or hamster died? Her family members are fighting, terminally ill, or going through a rough time? It could be anything.

"Where's your mom or your dad? Are you alone?" I ask, a little worried.

"My dad is at home," she replies, pointing across the street at a run-down apartment building. So I guess she's not lost. And I'm assuming her dad knows she's here?

"Oh, okay. Well, that really sucks, that you're not feeling good," is the most astute thing I can think of. Then, "Is there anything I can do to help? Like maybe...do you want someone to talk to? I'm Erin, by the way. And this is my dog, Bruce." I glance down at him; he looks bored but companionable and potentially comforting to a small child.

This time, the kid doesn't even look up at me, but I hear a gentle "Okay." She sniffles.

I crouch down a respectful distance away from her. "I don't mean to be weird or creepy or anything like that," I continue. Is that something a weird or creepy person would say? "I mean, when I was a kid like you, I had a lot of things to say but hardly anyone to tell it to." Just thinking about my childhood makes me want to gag.

The little girl doesn't even bat an eye. Maybe I should try to be more relatable. "Am I boring you? Okay, what about this, then? I'll tell you what's on my mind, and then you can tell me something about yourself, if you want to. Here, you can even pet Bruce the whole time, if you want." Bruce admittedly doesn't seem enthused by the prospect of being tossed off to a stranger, but I have a good feeling about this girl. I want to prove to myself that I'm still capable of making people feel better.

She lifts her head just slightly, resting her chin on her forearms and staring at me. "Fine, but I want to go first." I can't believe I got her to speak an entire sentence to me. Amazing.

I give her a corny thumbs-up. "Deal. But before you start, would you mind telling me your name? It can even be a fake one; I wouldn't know. Just something I can call you." This could be fun. I don't remember the last time I struck up a conversation with a stranger.

"Natalia," she says, with an air of grandness that doesn't seem to fit with the fact that she's so young. She wipes her nose on her butterfly-patterned long-sleeve shirt.

"Hi, Natalia. So, what's up? What's got you feeling so sad right now?" I try to appear sincere and genuine; I do feel sincere and genuine, but does that really mean anything if she doesn't perceive it that way?

"My dad, he told me all the polar bears are dying…" She starts sobbing again, absorbing the pain of an entire species in her four feet of height. It's actually not too far off from the "my dog died" catastrophe I was expecting to hear.

"Yeah…I feel you, Nat. Hearing about stuff like that is… not fun," I sputter, trying to buy myself time to think of something helpful to offer. I must be able to think of something that would strike a chord. I close my eyes for a moment, trying to concentrate. "You really empathize, don't you?"

"What's 'empathize' mean?" she asks flatly, her tone reminding me that she's not here for a vocab lesson.

"It means like…feeling what other people are feeling," I reply.

Her brow furrows. "What? Like with superpowers or magic?"

"No, it's more just…pretend? You know what the other person is probably feeling because you've been in a similar situation before, too. You care about them and are connected to them somehow, so you start to feel what they're feeling." Natalia holds my gaze for a moment and then shrugs, seeming uninterested in the concept. I guess if what you have on your mind is the ramifications of global climate change, everything else takes a back seat.

We watch a few birds and squirrels scamper around the field. I run my hand through my unwashed hair. I don't know what else to add, and I'm about to call it quits, but then she asks, "So, is it a good thing or a bad thing? Empathy." Her dark-brown eyes shine with vulnerability.

Oh, hell. What would Ethel say if she were in this situation? "Well, in your case, it might not be so helpful. Because it seems like it's really putting a damper on your day, making you feel sad, I mean." She nods solemnly. "But you know, it's important to care, even when it hurts, because that's what'll give you the strength, the power, to do something about it."

Having dozed off sometime in the past few minutes, Bruce rolls over in his sleep, toward Nat, and she scoots over to him and strokes his back. I decide to change the subject to ask for her child wisdom. "Hey Nat, mind if I ask you a question?"

"That's a question already," she replies with a cheeky grin that only someone her age could get away with.

"Yeah, okay. So, here's my real question: what do you think your perfect world would look like?"

"Anything I can imagine?" she asks. She stomps her feet and her Velcro shoes light up.

"Anything you can imagine."

"There would be a lot of pizza and ice cream. But eating it, even a lot of it every day, wouldn't make you sick. And there would be plenty. And I would live in this awesome castle in the sky with happy polar bears." She smiles and I see her adorable, crooked teeth.

I love how easy it is for her to imagine this world. To know what she wants, or at least, to think she knows what she wants—and isn't that all that matters? "So why do you want those things? Pizza and ice cream, for example."

"Because they're yummy!" Obviously.

"And why do you like that they're yummy?"

"What? Well, whenever I eat them, I feel...happy."
Of course.

"So basically, in your perfect world, you would feel happy?"
In my perfect world, I would be my best self. I'd be learning tons of shit and building really cool stuff. I'd be unstoppable.

"Yeah, I guess," she replies patiently, probably accustomed to getting interrogated by adults.

Then suddenly, she frowns. "But would my dad be there? And Grandma? And Lisa and Emily? They're my best friends. And Fluffy and Corduroy? They're my cats."

"Well, would you want them to be?" I try to keep my voice neutral. "Do they make you happy?"

She's about to nod, but then she hesitates. "Well, sometimes, my friends really get on my nerves. Or my dad talks about things that make me cry or my cats take my stuff without asking." She scratches her nose and stares off into the distance, thinking. "But I would want them to be there with me because I love them. I think they do make me happy, just in a different way than pizza and ice cream."

"Of course." My simulation wasn't a place where everyone was happy all the time and everything went smoothly; there was struggle and there was pain, like there is here.

But in my simulation, unlike in the real world, I knew every bad thing came with a good thing that outweighed it. I knew there was a reason for everything and in the end, it would all be worth it. But here, my heartache is just heartache, and my grief is just grief. Nothing good comes from it.

My eyes start watering. The only reason I was ever able to deal with this chaotic and senseless world was because I didn't know what the alternative felt like. Now that I've been through my simulation, I can't readjust myself to this world. I start sobbing. I did this to myself.

Nat crawls over to me and gently pats me on the shoulder. "Why are you crying?" But I can't bring myself to look her in the eye.

"I'm sorry, Nat, but I need to go." I allow myself to give her a quick hug before I run off, leaving Bruce asleep with her.

I need to go back to the one place where I still belong. I don't know if there will still be that soul-sucking all-consuming glitch thing, but I have to try.

23

___

It's just over a two-mile run to the lab from the park. I know this because of all the running I've done in the past several months, as part of my stupid quest to become like Ethel. But since I've reverted back to my old self for the past few weeks, I'm not in shape anymore. My lungs heave and my heart feels like it's beating out of my chest.

But I can't stop now. My plan is to stay in the simulation indefinitely. If all goes well, my consciousness will never have to return to the real world. Even if someone finds my body, they won't be able to get my mind back from the simulated reality. In the real world, I'll be in a comatose state, and when my physical body dies of hunger or thirst or whatever, then so be it.

Dodging a man on an electric scooter, I turn left to take a shortcut through one of the bad parts of town, down a street that I used to avoid because it smells like piss and cigarette smoke. I almost trip several times as I sprint over the uneven sidewalk. I start to jay walk across the street when an oncoming car honks at me.

"Fucking hell," I mutter. I need to get to lab before I change my mind about this. I backtrack the few steps to the sidewalk and press the button to cross the street instead. I wait anxiously, adrenaline still coursing through my veins.

Behind me, I hear a hacking cough. I turn and see an old woman with matted blond hair sitting on the sidewalk a few feet away from me. She's leaning against the graffitied wall of the abandoned shop building, a ragged blue sleeping bag at her feet. She stares blankly ahead, like she's in her own world. I hadn't noticed her before.

I turn back around so as not to stare, but I wonder: how long has she been sitting in that spot today? How long has she been living on the streets? What got her here in the first place, what were the events that led up to this point in her life? Who was it who let her down? What would her life have been like if this or that variable had been different? What would her simulation world look like? If she had the choice, would she choose to experience it, forever?

When the walk sign comes on, I shake away those thoughts and run across the street. After a half dozen more blocks and three turns, I pass the vine-covered metal fence to the botanical garden, the one that used to be a central part of my morning routine. I cut through the center of campus, where my lab is located.

The ground is littered with old flyers promoting events and clubs. I sprint past a kid with a Spikeball set and a volleyball, past a young couple holding hands and laughing together. With every step, I take in my surroundings for what may be the last time. I race past the imposing brick buildings of the school of medicine and the school of music. The campus bookstore, the rec center, the sports stadium, the library, the dorms and the dining halls, the classroom buildings.

It's happening. I'm really doing this. For a moment, I wonder if I will miss this place, but then I remember: when I go back to the simulation, I won't have a memory of this world at all. I will have nothing to miss.

When I finally get to the gray front door of the lab, my chest is heaving so intensely I'm afraid I'll collapse. But I can't now, not when I'm so close. My head is spinning, and I slap my face to try to recenter myself. I lie faceup on a wooden bench a few feet away, resting my arms on my stomach. I focus on my breathing.

Whenever I'm faced with a decision about whether or not to do something big, I'm always biased toward doing it. If I choose not to take the leap, I have to keep choosing that every day for the rest of my life because I could always change my mind. On the other hand, if I decide to take the leap, once I've done it, there's no going back. I want the freedom that comes with that kind of closure.

After a few minutes, my pulse stabilizes. I slowly stand and peek through the big glass window of the lab's main space. The blinds are half open, and I can make out the backs of two heads facing the whiteboard wall. I squint. It's Yuna and Sean, the two most chill grad students in the lab. They're focused on their conversation, as they usually are, making energetic hand gestures to illustrate their points. I'm in luck; they'll make this easy.

I have a feeling I look insane, barging into work in my athletic shorts and T-shirt, which were old and dirty to begin with and are also graced with dog fur from Bruce and sweat from my run over here. I certainly feel delirious, but it is what it is.

I paste a smile on my face. I'll play it cool and make it quick. I knock on the door before entering. Yuna and Sean turn to face me at the same time.

"Oh, hey Erin!" Yuna says, capping the black dry erase marker in her hand. "What's up? Come in."

I make eye contact with her briefly without breaking my pace. "Hey, I'd love to, but I actually gotta step into the VR room for a second. I just had an epiphany on my run this morning. Really can't wait to try it out, you know what I mean?" Being overly enthusiastic about your job is always socially acceptable and can get you out of almost any situation.

I get the sense that Yuna knows something's up though—I haven't come into lab on the weekend for the past month—but she also knows that I'd want her to play along with it. I love her that way. I nod at Sean and walk past the two, stepping over papers strewn on the floor and avoiding stray chairs. Will they miss me? Maybe, but they'll be okay.

I step inside the VR room and wait for the door to click shut behind me. The bright white walls of the room make me feel nauseous. The enormous computer hums softly before me. All these months of research and development with this machine, and now I'm going to be part of it.

As I go through the routine of uploading all my new personal data to the program, I remind myself that I'm just doing the best I can, as I always have. Before the simulation, I had no guiding light, no North Star to head toward; after the simulation, I did, and I tried to reach it—I really tried—but I found that I couldn't. Not because of some failure on my part, but simply because no matter how hard I try, this world can never let me live the optimal life I led in the simulation. I'm not giving up on life; I'm just making my next best move.

On the monitor, the loading bar reaches 100 percent. I feel my adrenaline pumping as I scan through the report. Satisfied, I shakily reach for the headset and secure it into place. The black adjustable strap feels so familiar to me between my sweaty palms. It's ready and I'm ready. The final systems check comes out clear. I place my cursor on the green play button on the top left corner. As I click it, I can almost feel the millions of signals activating and traveling from one place to another, making calculations to account for every single variable of the simulation. The fans start whirring and the startup sequence begins.

There's nothing to be sad about, nothing to be nervous about, nothing to be afraid of. I've done this before, and I know I want to do it again. This is it.

PART III

24

I wait to be transported back to my ideal existence. But then I keep waiting. And waiting.

Nothing happens.

I don't understand. I rip off the headset and lunge toward the computer. Did I screw something up? I feel like crying, but I start debugging.

First, the console output. Everything looks fine. Green "OK" messages printed across the screen; my new data uploaded, processed, the simulation successfully generated, the headset turned on and running the simulation. What the hell?

Next step: the code. Is there anything wrong with the code itself? That wouldn't make sense. It's the same code I used last time...The headset? No, nothing's changed since last time.

Oh. Is it something to do with the "glitch" I experienced the first time I ran the simulation? But I fed the code my new data; could there really be *another* problem in the system that made this happen a *second* time? This should be a clean run.

And even if there was something that caused another "glitch," why would it make the system not even start?

My pulse races. I don't know what to do. I glance through the code, and I try making some changes to it, testing them, and seeing if they make a difference, but they don't. A blank screen. What else can I do? Look for a solution on the internet? I don't even know what I would put in the search query bar. I can ask someone for help. Yuna and Sean? No, I can't face them now.

I lie back against the wall and curl into a ball. I can't accept that this won't work. I can't. I'm not ready for that. Now that I've experienced the ideal world I want to live in, I can't go back to living in this god-awful world where I'm lost and alone and broken. Things just *worked* in the simulation, things felt *right* there, *I* felt right there.

There is nothing here for me anymore. Joel is gone. My dream for a new career is gone. Abi is basically gone to me. I put all this effort into becoming my best self, and now I don't feel anything like myself.

I close my eyes and think for a moment. Why am I getting so worked up about this? I'm an adult. Why am I acting like a five-year-old who wants to keep playing pretend? I've gone through every hard thing in my life that I didn't think I would get through. What's different this time? Why am I being so weak?

It's because I felt the alternative. I can no longer see the real world for what it is; I see it for what it isn't—every single way it doesn't measure up to my simulated reality.

Suddenly, I hear a knock on the door, snapping me back to the present. Sean's voice says, "Hey, Erin? You good? Yuna and I are wrapping up and we're heading out."

I find it in me to reply, "Yeah, thanks. See you later." Despite my best efforts, my voice is a bit hoarse.

I wait for pushback from Sean, but there is none. I did want to be left alone, but part of me also wanted him to notice I was lying because that'd show he really knew me. But he doesn't.

I lie faceup on the floor and stare at the white ceiling. It's plain. Empty. Terrifying. I close my eyes. I'm not sure if I fell asleep, but sometime later, I'm startled by the creak of the door opening. Who? How? I open my eyes. It takes a moment for them to adjust.

It's Isa, with her yellow cleaning cart. I didn't know she came on weekends. I don't have time to put up some semblance of normalcy but still, I scramble into a cross-legged seat on the carpet and run a hand through my knotted hair.

This time, there is no denying that I am going through something. There is nowhere to hide, and that floods me with relief. Isa sees me, raw. She stands there, staring at me for a moment. She leaves the cleaning cart behind her. "Erin? What happened?" she asks, surprised.

I look down at my hands. They're trembling. I don't know where to start. Anything I think of saying just sounds stupid. I feel Isa looking at me tight-lipped. I know the bags under her eyes and the stiffness of her joints didn't come from an easy life, and I feel ashamed of myself.

"I don't want to be here anymore..." My voice is wobbly and pitiful. "There's this fake world that I made," I gesture toward the headset, "and it has everything I want, but it's... it's not working. I don't know what's wrong." I must seem out of my mind.

She takes a seat in the desk chair, carrying herself elegantly like the matriarch she is. "And why can't you stay in *this* world?" she asks, setting her rough hands on her lap. "What is it that you are not strong enough to handle?" She pauses. "Nothing."

We sit in silence for a time before Isa gently asks, "Can I tell you something?" I don't react, but I'm listening. "Look at me." Reluctantly, I meet her gaze.

"I don't think this…other world you are talking about…I don't think there is anything wrong with it. I think it is working just fine. It is telling you that you need to stay here. With your family and friends. Because even though you don't like it all the time, this is your home."

I burst into tears. Maybe she's right.

25

———

Four months. It's been four months since I tried reentering the simulation and failed. Settling into a comfortable spot on a flat rock near the edge of the sea cliff, I realize that a lot has changed since then. I slip my cold and clammy hands into the front pocket of my thrifted hoodie. The sky and the ocean reflect serene blue-black hues onto each other, and I can tell they're getting brighter by the minute, heralding the sunrise. I could sit here forever, alone with my thoughts—I could stare out into the horizon until I went blind. If I remember correctly, this wasn't like the ocean in my simulation at all. Or maybe it's just that my *perception* of the ocean was completely different when I was Ethel? Maybe both.

I check my analog watch. I hadn't planned on coming early, not at all; I'd wanted to get a good night's sleep. But when I randomly woke up at four-thirty this morning, I thought, why not? In an hour, I'm driving back home to pick up Abi and Bruce, who'd by some miracle found his way back home after I ditched him at the park, for a morning hike. We figured if he's going to die soon, we might as well give him a taste of the good life, to bring him along on our outings. So, when we stumbled upon a used stroller at our neighbor's garage sale, I had an idea. A week later, we had ourselves a doggy stroller custom-made for our doggo using duct tape and random recyclables we had around the house. Startup culture did teach me how to be scrappy, and I'm grateful for that. This will be our first time trying out the doggy stroller in the wild. I can't wait.

I won't pretend that everything is back to sunshine and roses between Abi and me, but we've been having some pretty heart-to-heart conversations for the past few weeks. I've been working on proving that I'm different this time around. I want to become someone who's willing to meet the people I love where they are, to work with them through our inconvenient-but-manageable incompatibilities, because they're worth it to me. Abi has been patient with me, and she's told me that our friendship is worth it to her.

I breathe in the salty air and gaze into the expanse of the water. There are a lot of ways to think about the ocean, to try to process it, because there's a lot that the ocean can symbolize. Persistence, for one: the constant rhythm of the waves and shift of the tide. Permanence: the water before me is the same water that's been on this Earth since water first became a thing. Oblivion: what becomes of a wave once it disappears back into the ocean surface? Purification: the way the tide comes in and washes away all that it touches (or would that be destruction?). The power of collective action: combine billions of droplets of water, and you have yourself a giant body of water.

There is so much to see. I bend down and run my fingers over the bumpy dry dirt, trailing behind a tiny red ladybug next to a patch of violet wildflowers. What other species call this place home? After several minutes of close examination, I'm proud to have witnessed a black beetle, a fat gray pill bug, a couple of squirmy dirt-brown millipedes, and a green plant hopper.

Thousands of blades of grass poke out of the crevices in the dry, tightly packed dirt. Behind me are bushes with green leaves of all different shapes and sizes. A tree's branches curl and bend organically in the wind, its gray-brown bark so textured that I see its crevices from a dozen feet away. The base of the trunk slopes outward, burrowing the tree's roots deep into the earth. Down the slope of the cliff, the thick layer of vegetation gives way to reddish-tan streaks of sediment.

What is the story behind this particular place? How many others have sat in this very spot? What does the future hold for it? What part do I play in all of that? I feel so lucky to bear witness to this sliver of land, and I want to see it for all of its depth and beauty.

Also, it's my birthday tomorrow! Normally, I don't make a big deal about it, but this one's going to be special. I have a dinner reservation with my parents at my favorite Thai place on Sawtelle. I really don't know how it'll go, this being the first time we've all gotten together in months, but I've resolved to stop being angry at them for not being there for me, for not being exactly who I wanted or needed them to be when I was growing up. I want to try being close with them again, not because I think it'll work—in fact, given that my neural net kept me so distant from my family in the simulation, it probably won't—but just for the sake of trying. Just because I want to.

As for the lab, last month, I apologized profusely for checking out of my lab duties, and everyone was supportive and understanding about it. I'm even working on a new paper about my simulation experiment, and I think it'll be a good one. I'm slowly but surely learning to forgive myself, for stupidly dropping the ball on my day job in the name of going "all in" on getting my simulation's engineering career. I think I'd been happy where I was, and the only reason I started feeling like I needed a change was because the simulation told me so.

Though I will admit, I am still casually looking at engineering jobs in the startup scene, but I no longer feel like it's my moral duty to seek one out. What's more, I want to be part of the diversity and inclusion efforts; even if engineering isn't part of my path, I want it to make it better for those whose it is.

Realizing that my eyes have gotten dry from all this staring out into the abyss, I squeeze them shut, focusing on the feeling of the eddies of the wind dovetailing around my body. It's cold and crisp; I like it. My bangs whip into my face and when I brush them aside, they feel slightly damp. My head's been misted by the ocean breeze, like some kind of anointment or baptism.

Is that You, God, in the whisper of the wind? I think, partly kidding and partly not. *What do You think of me now?* That's another thing: now, I go to church every once in a blue moon. I still can't bring myself to really believe, but I have some church friends, and I like their values and whatnot. Every time I see the church building, I'm reminded of Joel, and it hurts, but I'm coming to terms with his passing.

As I open my eyes, I place my palms behind me and lean back against them. I'm tired, but I'm happy. Should I try my hand at painting seascapes? I don't know how it's even possible to paint water realistically, but I don't have to paint it realistically. I mean, where would we be if we only judged the value of art by how closely it resembled what we see with our eyes? We have our eyes for that.

Besides, if you really try to take it all in, to comprehend the vastness of the water and every crash of the waves, you will only become aware of how much you're missing. I actually think that having this loss of resolution is better than having some perfect replica neatly packed into a jar. Because the part that gets lost in translation, that's the part it's up to you to create, to experience the ocean in your own context. The process of perception is a creative and personal one.

A pair of seagulls glide across my field of view and my chapped lips curl into a smile. In our session yesterday, Zoey asked me, after all this, what is it that I think about my secret experiment? Well, in hindsight, I needed it. In order to figure out what truly matters to me, I had to experience the life I thought I wanted, then see it fall apart for some unknown reason, and finally fail to recreate it in my real life. I'm glad I saw it through.

Zoey also asked me, *what now?* I've toyed with the idea of going off the grid, completely abandoning modern society, joining a self-sufficient cooperative living community, taking up subsistence farming. Never exchanging currency again, never knowing the time except by looking up at the position of the sun in the sky.

These ideas are alluring and glamorous. But they're not what I'm looking for. Because I do not think a different place will change me. It's as they say, "wherever you go, there you are." In fact, I think what I'm looking for, I already have. Friends and enemies, family and strangers, meaning and chaos. I just need to see it.

All things considered, glitches, despite their negative connotation, might have been the best thing that could have happened to me. Dare I say, the optimal—wait. My breath catches.

All this time, I'd been trying to figure out why the simulation code malfunctioned so as to generate something like the "glitch." I kept searching for some kind of explanation as to what went wrong, but what if nothing went wrong? Because the more I think about it, I don't think the "glitch" was a mistake at all. What if it was intentional, part of the system's plan all along?

Realizing that existence must be the most poignant algorithm of all, I rise to my feet and resume my function as Erin.

ACKNOWLEDGMENTS

———

From the bottom of my heart, thank you for making the publication of *The Glitch* possible. Each of you had an impact on the writing of this book, whether you were my teacher, mentor, family member, friend, family friend, or someone who didn't know me personally but who believed in my dream nonetheless. It's been an honor to have you on board and I hope that I made you proud.

Abel Rangel Espinosa
Addie Chong
Alexander Chang
Anjelika Amog
Ariya Amin
Arlene Biala
Ava Asmani
Ayesha Kumbhare
Brett Bymaster
Briana Fowler
Caitlin P. Stanton
Calvin Booke

Carey Nachenberg
Carla Collins
Cate Galloway
Catherine Yeo
Celena Nijmeh
Chesung Ryu
Chris Fong
Clare Chung
Cody King
Colleen Lemon
Colleen McDonough
Corinne Takara

Daria Rouhbakhsh
Della Speer
Dennis Briggs
Dorothy Balkon
Edmund B. Allen
Elaine Wu
Eliot Huang
Eric Koester
Fred Chu
Gabby Brown
Gabriel McAdams
Glenda Yap
Hanna Newlin
Hyunhee Kim
Ian Do
Isabella Vasquez
Isabelle Le
Jacqueline Paredes-Kao
Jason Dufenhorst
Jean Yi
Jenna Miri Kim
Jerry Herskovitz
Jill Pantig
Jineel Joshi
Jingtao Xia
Joanna Kim
Joanne Cheung
Joe B. Rodriguez
Joy Liu
Julia Sargis
Jung Park
Kaela Son

Karis Do
Karla Furstenberg
Katherine Kim
Kathleen T. Quint
Katy Castañeda-LaMar
Krisha Minocha
Lara Levy
Laura Bald
Lauren McCawley
Lauren McLane
Leslie Kim
Linh Bauer
Lisa Hisamura
Lisa Le
Lourdes Andrade-Torres
Lucas Simone
Lucila Castillo
Madison Odam
Maimuna Syed
Mary Jessie Celestin
Mason Do
Matthew Park
Max Kwon
Mel Sarmento
Mia Giacinto
Michael Burrell
Michaela Harrel
Michelle Kim
Nadin Tamer
Namching Young
Natalia Luzuriaga
Nikki Woo

Noah Steffler
Pancho Chang
Peter Glasser
Rachel Kong
Rishi Sankar
Robin Dewis
Ronald Dunn
Rosa Isela Coss
Ruby Barajas
Russell Chough
Sarah Nichols
Sarah Wilen
Satoru Isaka
Sean Patrick Kelker
Shana Chen

Shirlene Lau
Shreyas Kulkarni
Shysel Granados
Spurthi Rallapalli
Steven Boyd
Sudarshan Seshadri
Tammy Hu
Tammy Turnipseed
Thomas La Plante
Tim Koring
Tyler Pena
Yong Kwon
Zoey Wang
Zohreh Moaven

Thank you to my sources of inspiration; your words transformed my understanding of myself and of the world, and my writing follows in your footsteps.

Jenny Odell
Anna Wiener
Jia Tolentino

Thank you to the folks at Creator Institute and New Degree Press for helping me through the highs and lows of this adventure.

Mozelle Jordan
David Grandouiller
Amy Dong
Haley Newlin

John Saunders
Tasslyn Magnusson
Eric Koester

Finally, a few special shoutouts: Thank you Joy, for filling my life with laughter and good content for my writing. Thank you Sud, for not canceling me and for being excited about my ideas. Thank you Jingtao, Mr. Isaka, and Caitlin, for your continual mentorship and encouragement. Thank you to my family; your love has turned me into the person I am today.